Derivatives
for
Decision Makers

Derivatives
for
Decision Makers

Strategic Management Issues

George Crawford and Bidyut Sen

JOHN WILEY & SONS, INC.

New York • Chichester • Brisbane • Toronto • Singapore

This text is printed on acid-free paper.

Copyright © 1996 by George Crawford and Bidyut Sen
Published by John Wiley & Sons, Inc.

Library of Congress Cataloging-in-Publication Data:
Crawford, George
    Derivatives : strategic management issues / George Crawford
    and Bidyut Sen.
        p.   cm.
    Includes index.
    ISBN 0-471-12994-1 (cloth : alk. paper)
    1. Derivative securities—United States.   I. Sen, Bidyut.
    II. Title.
    HG6024.U6C7   1996
    332.84'5—dc20

Printed in the United States of America

10 9 8 7 6 5 4 3 2 1

Financial Dedication to Fiduciary Foundation

All of the authors' financial proceeds from writing this book have been dedicated to the Fiduciary Foundation, a charitable foundation with a mission to educate and assist the fiduciaries who control much of the wealth of the world through pension, corporate, mutual fund, charitable, and private trusts. The authors hope that this book itself, and the activities of the Foundation, will permit fiduciaries to better fulfill their duties, for the greater good of their beneficiaries and of all people.

Personal Dedication

The authors dedicate this book to their families, with love and appreciation.

Contents

Foreword

Directors or decision makers need to know about derivatives. A world of information on the subject has been distilled into this comprehensive and understandable book, which offers food for thought to novices and experts alike. I would expect nothing less of the authors, in view of their own wealth of practical experience and theoretical insight.

Those seeking a clear explanation of the basics of derivatives, and of their application to simple and complex situations, will find this book invaluable. It provides new insights and understanding to executives, investors, portfolio managers, traders, and those who have merely heard about the subject and want to have some broad understanding of the implications of the widespread use of derivatives in their pension funds and mutual funds. I am sure that regulators and legislators also will benefit by reading this book.

While I was chairman of the Securities and Investments Board in the United Kingdom, I came to realize that derivatives can be dangerously misunderstood by both users and regulators, but that, properly understood, they provide a set of tools that can be used both safely and effectively. Wise legislative and regulatory approaches must be based on a clear understanding of the issues by regulators and legislators themselves. I hope they will include this book in their reading.

Members of boards of financial institutions and other businesses that are now using derivatives need to understand the subject themselves, at least well enough to ensure that appropriate policies are adopted and rigorously implemented. They cannot afford to turn these responsibilities wholly over to others, as many chief executives and directors have learned to their chagrin.

Despite the great seriousness and importance of its purpose, this book is also very enjoyable. There are anecdotes that entertain as well as instruct, graphs that clearly illustrate key points and complex transactions, very practical tips on avoiding embarrassing losses and legal liabilities, and even some provocative conjecture about what the future may hold. I commend this book most warmly.

SIR DAVID WALKER

Preface

People who manage other people's money, or who through a chain of command have any authority over such managers, need to have some understanding of derivatives since most businesses and investment managers are using them today. If you are a corporate manager or director, pension fiduciary, bank trustee, or in any other capacity responsible for managing money, we wrote this book for you. Even if the only money you manage is that on which you and your family depend, or if you have given other people the authority to manage your money, this book contains important knowledge. So many businesses and investment managers are using derivatives today that no one with any responsibility for money should be functioning without a basic understanding of derivatives. That knowledge is absolutely essential for safety in today's financial environment.

No knowledge of derivatives is assumed at the outset of this book: The basic derivatives (options, futures, swaps, and financially engineered products) are explained, along with the markets in which they are used, and the uses to which they can be put.

This book will show you how derivatives can be used to limit business risks, or to insure your investments against loss, all at a price and with a deductible, just like an insurance policy. The book will also show you how derivatives can be used to seek high profits, at high risk. When you have responsibility for other people's money, either directly or through a chain of command, you need to know the level of risk you are willing to undertake so that if those risks result in losses—as they sometimes inevitably will—the size of those losses will not come as a complete and unwelcome surprise.

We will also discuss the different kinds of business risks and how they can be hedged with derivatives. Many examples demonstrate ways to hedge business or investment risks, and ways to use derivatives for business and investment, with greater or lesser levels of risk.

This book will also explain lessons to be learned from recent disasters reported in the press concerning derivatives, so that you and those working under you or managing your money don't repeat those mistakes. It will describe how derivative disasters tend to engulf everyone up the chain of command to the very top, so that they can ruin the careers even of those very remote from the particular decisions which backfired. Policies, supervision, and controls to prevent such disasters will also be described.

Finally, we take a look into the future. The use of derivatives has grown spectacularly in recent years, to a point where it is a dominant presence in the world financial system—and these uses are still evolving. A great deal remains unsettled concerning derivatives, and the future is always a mystery, but it is sure to include fascinating developments in this field.

Acknowledgments

The authors appreciate the assistance of colleagues and friends at Morgan Stanley and Stanford Law School, which made this book possible. The very capable work of Matthew Behrent was of great help in all aspects of the book. Members of the Derivatives Products Group at Morgan Stanley, students in the Fiduciary Investing class at Stanford Law School, faculty including Professor Joe Grundfest, the former SEC Commissioner, and Hoover Institution scholars all provided a stimulating sounding board for the ideas underlying the book. Skillful assistance on particular research topics, transaction examples, figures, and the glossary was provided by many, to whom we are most grateful. Special thanks to our assistants who were so generous with their personal time in helping us with the manuscript. The authors also appreciate the many suggestions of colleagues as to the contents and coverage of the book, including those of Bob McCabe, who, as a director of four New York Stock Exchange companies, first pointed out his need for a book such as this.

The authors gratefully acknowledge the invaluable help they have received, but accept the ultimate responsibility for any errors, and indeed reserve the right to modify their own views as this rapidly changing field unfolds.

Introduction

Derivatives can be used as risk management tools or as investment alternatives. They can be used with or without leverage and with or without exposure beyond the amount of the investment. Investing in derivatives can be just as safe as any other form of investing. In fact, it can be much safer. Or it can be very risky, but provide the opportunity for much higher returns. It all depends on the investor's choice.

You are probably using derivatives right now, even if you are unaware of it. We said this to the head of one of the United States' largest pension funds, and he immediately denied it. Then we asked if his pension fund had any investments in foreign stocks. He replied that it did. We asked if the pension fund ever hedged against the foreign currency risk involved in foreign stocks. He said that it did, and we pointed out that the fund was using currency futures and forwards to do so, a form of derivative. This was a very intelligent, highly sophisticated executive, often quoted in the *Wall Street Journal* on important subjects. He just didn't think what he was doing involved derivatives, since it was *decreasing* the riskiness of his pension fund's investments, rather than *increasing* it.

If you have a home mortgage, you are probably using derivatives—to your benefit. In fact, your home mortgage may be full of derivatives. For example, it may contain a provision that allows

1

you to pay it off at any time, without any prepayment penalty. This gives you an *option* to prepay your loan, which is to your great advantage if interest rates go down and you want to refinance. You have a loan with an *embedded option*, which is a form of derivative. As another example, if you have a variable rate mortgage, the rate itself is probably derived from a common index such as the London interbank offered rate (LIBOR), or 11th district cost-of-funds index (COFI), which is the cost of funds charged by the Federal Reserve Bank in the 11th district. There may also be a limit on the increase in interest rates you pay, such as "the interest rate charged may not increase more than 1 percent in any six-month period." Or, there may be another limitation on interest rate increases over the life of the loan, such as "the interest rate charged may never exceed 10 percent per annum." Both of these provisions are *caps*, which are common in derivative instruments.

The purpose of this book is to help you use derivatives wisely by understanding derivatives and their application well enough to ask the right questions of yourself and your trusted advisers. Derivatives come in many forms, simple or complex, but you do not have to be a financial engineer with degrees in advanced mathematics to ask the right questions and decide whether a particular use of derivatives is right for you or your company.

FIDUCIARIES AND DERIVATIVES

Those responsible for investing other people's money are fiduciaries under the law. As such, it is their duty to balance the risk and reward of each potential investment and of all the portfolio investments as a group. The directors and top executives of the company have a supervisory responsibility over this function, just as they have a supervisory responsibility over the management and control of risks in all other areas of the business.

Of course, people with this responsibility cannot avoid taking some risks with the money in their care. Even risk-free investments in U.S. Treasury obligations can result in losses if the investment time is for a period that ends earlier or later than the maturity date. Investments in long-term Treasury bonds, backed by the full faith and credit of the United States, with no risk of default and absolute certainty that each payment of interest and principal will be timely made, lost about half their value from

1976 to 1981, as market interest rates rose and the present value of that future stream of certain cash payments declined.

The job is not to avoid risk altogether—an impossibility—but to strike a balance between risk and return that is suitable for the particular circumstances. The decision to invest in derivatives is like any other investment decision, and fiduciaries must understand the risks and rewards of the derivative investments they make. Derivatives may also be used to manage the risk and reward of other investments and business decisions. Fiduciaries must understand not only the risks and rewards of derivatives themselves, but also their use in the modern business world as an investment strategy and for risk management.

FOUR USES OF DERIVATIVES

Balancing risk and reward is necessary with or without derivatives. Adding derivatives to the picture provides another tool, or step, in the balancing process. Derivatives can be used in four basic ways:

- *Derivatives can be used as a convenient substitute for other investments, leaving risk and reward unchanged.* For example, instead of buying each of the stocks in the Standard & Poor's index of the 500 largest U.S. stocks, a pension fund might buy an S&P 500 futures contract of the same face value and set aside the full value in cash reserves. This strategy is no more or less risky than buying the stocks themselves, but uses futures as an efficient medium for investments.
- *Derivatives can be used to hedge other investments, reducing risk and reward, or to manage the risks inherent in a business.* For example, a pension fund that owns $1 billion of large U.S. stocks, but fears that a temporary market decline is imminent, might sell $1 billion of futures contracts, or buy $1 billion of put options, to protect its portfolio against the risk of a general market decline.
- *Derivatives can be used speculatively to increase risk and reward through leverage.* For example, an investor with $1 million could buy futures contracts with a face, or *notional*, value equal to $10 million of stock. This investor is taking a big risk in hope of a big gain, leveraging the investment approximately 10 to 1. If the stock market goes up 10 percent, increasing the value of the

stock to $11 million, then the investor has made a $1 million profit, doubling his or her $1 million investment. If the stock market goes down 10 percent, decreasing the value of the stock to $9 million, then all of the investor's money is lost.

- *Derivatives are also the basis for modern financial engineering.* For example, mortgage derivatives can be used to create a repackaged asset that is only a part of an underlying bundle of mortgages financially engineered into a variety of subdivided forms. One derivative might pass on only the interest payments of the underlying mortgages, for example, while another might pass on only the principal. These new investments may be more suitable for the needs of a particular investor than the underlying asset taken as a whole.

You, your pension fund, or a company in which you are a shareholder, director, or other decision maker is most likely using derivatives right now. Almost all financial institutions, such as banks, brokerages, and insurance companies, are doing so in one way or another, though few like to admit it in the present atmosphere of panic over derivatives, even if their particular uses are completely safe. Among financial institutions, a vast majority use derivatives internally as well as in products provided to their customers. Among nonfinancial companies, a recent survey indicates over one-third now admit to using derivatives—some commentators have suggested that many more should be. Perhaps your company or pension fund is already using them carefully or perhaps not. If it isn't using derivatives, perhaps it should be. The purpose of this book is to help you understand what derivatives are all about, which uses are safe, which are risky, and how to guard against the risks. It will also introduce you to the legal obligations of people who manage other people's money, how these relate to derivatives, and how derivatives may change these obligations.

Part 1

INTRODUCING DERIVATIVES

INTRODUCTION

Derivatives come in many varieties. Some are traded on organized exchanges, some are privately arranged. No one description fits them all, so almost any generalization about derivatives is, in some respect, inaccurate. It is much more useful to discuss particular investing or hedging strategies than to discuss derivatives in general.

Part 1 of the book will present a brief overview of three major types of derivatives: futures, options, and swaps. First is a discussion of *futures* and *options*, perhaps the oldest use of derivatives. These allow buyers and sellers to protect themselves against unpredictable price changes in the future or to speculate on these changes. Next, we look at the use of *swaps*, which is a way for a party to exchange the cash flows from an asset or liability by exchanging payments with a counterparty.

These three categories of derivatives can be used in the four ways described in the introduction: as a convenient proxy for the underlying investment; to hedge against another risk; as a free-standing investment; or to financially engineer an asset into a new investment device more suitable to the needs of the customer. To illustrate the latter, in chapter 3 we consider *mortgage derivatives*, in which portfolios of home mortgages are subdivided and repackaged in ways that are more useful to a variety of investors.

The use of leverage, an important factor in understanding derivatives, will be discussed at the end of part 1. Through leverage, a small amount of money can produce the same risks and rewards as a much larger amount. Leverage is a crucial attribute of many derivatives, and perhaps the most important concept of finance in general. Through the use of leverage, an investor can take greater risks—and reap greater rewards—than would otherwise be possible with an unleveraged investment. Leverage permits many Americans to make their largest single investment: the purchase of a home. Used properly, leverage also permits an investor to hedge other investments or risks without locking up a large amount of cash. However, leverage is also part of the cause of the disastrous losses that have been the subject of recent press: the Orange County disaster and the failure of Barings bank, for example.

As a fiduciary, you may not be responsible for understanding every detail of some of the derivative investments your organization may use, but if you understand leverage you will at least be aware of the extremes of risk and reward that the investment may entail.

1

Options
and Futures

THALES OF MILETUS:
OPTIONS AND FUTURES

The oldest reference to derivatives that we have seen appears in
the works of Aristotle, 2,400 years ago. He tells the story of a poor
philosopher named Thales, who was challenged with the ancient
question: "If you're so smart, why ain't you rich?" To demonstrate
that he could be rich if he were not spending so much time on his
main interest of philosophy, Thales used his knowledge of the
stars, the heavens, and the seasons to forecast that weather conditions would be right for a very successful olive crop in the coming
season. He then took what little money he had and went one by
one to the owners of the olive presses used to convert the olives
into oil. He made a small deposit to reserve each press for his
exclusive use during harvesttime. Having cornered the olive press
market in this way, Thales made the proverbial killing when the
harvest produced a bumper crop and olive presses were in such
high demand that Thales, as a monopolist, could charge whatever
he pleased. Now he was rich, and had answered the challenge.

In telling this story, Aristotle doesn't use the word *derivative* once. He doesn't need to, and the story is much easier to tell and to understand without the word. The contract was, however, no different than many modern derivatives: either an option or a future.

Under the terms of the contract, perhaps Thales' deposit gave him the right to use the olive presses, but not the obligation to use them. If he did use them, he would have to pay the rest of the rent. If he didn't, the owner of the press could simply keep the deposit and rent the press to someone else. This would be called an *option* on the olive presses, since it gives Thales the option to use and pay for the press, but doesn't require him to do so. However, the contract might have been slightly different. Perhaps it *required* Thales to pay for the olive presses come harvesttime, regardless of whether or not he wanted to use them at that time. If so, Thales' contract would be called a *future* or *forward*.

Although omitted by Aristotle, this difference would have been very important to Thales. Suppose Thales had been wrong about the weather forecast, the olive crop was a poor one, and there were more olive presses than people who wanted to use them. If Thales had only an option on the presses, and the harvest was bad, he would not rent the olive presses and would lose only his deposit. His contracts tying up the olive presses would have been worthless, but the deposit would be the extent of his loss. (See figure 1.1.) But if Thales had a forward or futures-type contract, and the harvest was bad, he would have been forced to rent the olive presses and would suffer a loss. He was already poor, and had used the last of his savings to tie up the olive presses. He would have been bankrupt if he had used futures contracts, and bankruptcy laws in the ancient world were much less lenient than they are today. He could have been thrown into debtor's prison, or perhaps sold into slavery. (See figure 1.2.)

Either way, Thales was using a form of derivative contract no different in concept or operation from the derivatives traded today on the futures exchanges, or arranged privately as Thales did. Aristotle's example is simply the oldest example we have been able to find so far. There are many other examples all through history, including the use of futures and options in the Renaissance by the famous Italian banking and merchant family, de'Medici, as well as the German Fuggers.

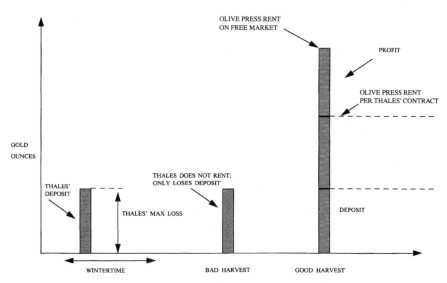

Figure 1.1   Thales' contract (option to rent).

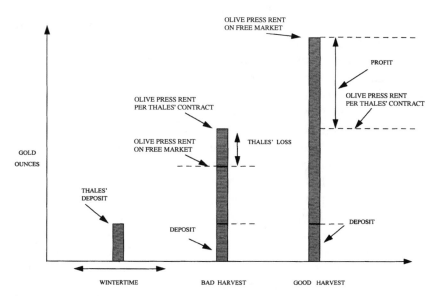

Figure 1.2   Thales' contract (must rent—forward or futures contract).

It should also be noted that whether Thales' contract was a future or an option, it would have involved leverage: Thales was gaining control of something with a large potential value by investing a small amount. From this point of view, the option contract seems preferable, but this preference comes at a price. The owner of the olive press will probably set a higher rent and require a higher deposit if he is not sure that the presses will actually be used at harvesttime. Leverage is discussed in detail in chapter 3.

HOW FUTURES MARKETS WORK

Forwards and options can be created through private contracts between buyer and seller (as did Thales). *Futures* and options can be traded on an open market. The oldest futures markets in the United States are in agricultural commodities, such as sugar, wheat, corn, hogs, and cattle. Today, by far the largest volume of trading is in financial futures—stocks and bonds. These commodity *exchanges* bring together producers and buyers of commodities looking to lock in future prices and speculators who are willing to take on the risk the producers and buyers wish to avoid. The exchanges mean modern-day Thales need not go door-to-door making individual contracts based on their predictions. The commodities are available in the form of standardized contracts: A set amount of the commodity can be purchased or sold for delivery on a specific date, months in the future. The commodity exchange and its member brokers also act as guarantors that all buyers or sellers will perform their obligations.

Suppose that Thales's contract was a futures contract and not an option. If so, the owners of the olive presses who entered the contracts were *hedgers:* By entering the contract, they were assuring themselves that they would receive the same rent from Thales, and make the same profit, whether the season was outstanding or terrible. A grain farmer who sells corn on the futures market does exactly the same thing today.

The commodity exchange makes it easy to attempt to profit from price changes or to hedge against them. Although commodity futures contracts provide for the actual delivery of the commodity at the closing date, very few purchasers have any intention of actually receiving delivery of thousands of pounds of live cattle, for example, on the delivery date specified in the contract. In fact, nearly 98 percent of the contracts to buy and sell futures are canceled before delivery, as buyers and sellers under the contracts simply pay one another, in cash through the exchanges, the economic value represented by the contracts. In some financial futures contracts (for example, the widely traded contracts based on the Standard & Poor's index of 500 stocks), no delivery is possible, and the parties are *required* to settle in cash, through the exchanges, as the contracts expire.

Physical delivery simply isn't necessary for most investment or hedging activities in the futures market. In only a few instances will even a commercial hedger actually require delivery of the commodity. Moreover, the standard contract may actually discourage delivery, since it allows the delivering party to specify the delivery spot, and the delivering party will certainly deliver commodities of no better quality than the minimum permitted under the contract. Rather than accept this delivery, the hedger can simply close out the contract, realizing its economic value in dollars, and purchase the goods on the cash market, through the customary, convenient channels.

For example, a corn farmer might sell a futures contract on the exchange at the beginning of the season for a quantity equivalent to the expected crop of corn. The farmer may then wait until a few days before the delivery date specified under the contract, sell the crop of corn to the usual buyers at market prices, and at the same time close out his or her futures contract. Suppose the farmer sells contracts at the beginning of the season for $30,000. Two days before the first date on which a buyer can require delivery, that contract might be selling for $50,000—there is a great demand for corn. There are now two choices. The farmer can hold the contract, accept the delivery notice, and deliver the corn under the contract for $30,000, going through somewhat burdensome formal delivery procedures. Alternatively, the farmer can *buy back* his or her contract for $50,000, absorbing a $20,000 loss on the contract but allowing sale of the corn at market prices for $50,000. On the other hand, if prices have fallen to $20,000, the farmer can either deliver the crops per the contract or sell the contract for a profit of $10,000 and sell the corn on the cash market for $20,000.

Whether the price of corn has gone up or down, and whether the farmer chooses to make delivery or close out the futures contract for cash, he or she gets around $30,000 for the corn, the price contracted for at the beginning of the season. The futures contract has allowed the hedger to lock in the sales price of his or her corn at the outset of the season.

Speculators in the futures market are even less prepared than hedgers for physical delivery, and will also close out their contracts before the contract terminates. Occasionally, however, certain large and sophisticated hedgers or speculators may decide that the rush of people closing out their contracts has pushed prices to unrealistic levels, and they will then make a profit by participating in physical delivery. It is the willingness of some traders to take advantage of these arbitrage opportunities that keeps prices close to those of the cash market, even at the end of the contract period.

LEVERAGE AND RISK CONTROL ON FUTURES EXCHANGES

The rules of most futures exchanges permit varying degrees of leverage. A small deposit in the present is sufficient to purchase the right to the entire contract in the future—this deposit is referred to as the *margin*. The leverage allowed is often as much as 20 to 1. A futures contract carries with it the risk of substantial losses—the leverage will increase the risk of large losses just as it increases the opportunity for large gains.

To ensure that every customer stands behind the financial obligations of his or her contracts, the exchange clearinghouse values each contract in every account at the end of each trading day and readjusts the cash balance of each trader's margin account accordingly. This is called *marking to market*, since the value of every contract is marked to the market price, and every trader is credited with any gains and debited with any losses in his or her account. The trader can remove from that account any cash resulting from these credits in excess of the margin requirements. Conversely, if the account is debited because of a loss of market value of his or her contracts, the trader must immediately deposit any cash or permissible collateral required to meet the margin. If the trader does not do so, his or her broker (called a *futures commission merchant* or *FCM*) may liquidate the account before the margin deposits are exhausted. If there is a negative balance in the account, the FCM must pay the exchange clearinghouse the difference, and try to collect it from the customer.

This daily marking to market ensures that all traders keep enough cash margin deposits in their accounts to cover the risks created by the high leverage of the contracts they have entered. When markets become highly volatile, the amount of margin deposit required for each contract can be and is increased substantially by the exchange. This protects every trader from running up debts far beyond the cash he or she has available. It also protects the system as a whole. If an FCM allows an individual investor to be tardy in depositing the required margin—contrary to exchange rules—so that adverse movements in price bankrupt the trader, the FCM itself is required to make up the difference daily through the clearinghouse. This exposure pressures the FCM to collect from the trader or liquidate his or her positions. FCMs are required by the exchanges to maintain minimum capital levels themselves, and in fact, few FCMs have failed. No futures exchange in this country has ever failed. Although investing through the futures exchanges can be risky, the risk of default is negligible.

TYPES OF FUTURES CONTRACTS

Futures exchanges exist for most major agricultural and industrial commodities, including crude oil, cotton, coffee, wheat, soybeans, copper, gold, silver, and the like. Financial futures are even more actively traded, including currency futures, Treasury bond futures, and stock-index-based futures. All of these contracts can be used for speculation and hedging. Currency futures can be used to hedge against or speculate upon foreign currency exposure. Treasury bond futures can be used to hedge against or speculate upon changes in interest rates. Index futures, such as the S&P 500, can be used to hedge a large private portfolio of stock or to speculate on market changes. Futures are also available based on a variety of more narrow indexes, such as an index of technology stocks.

FUTURES VERSUS FORWARDS

All futures contracts are traded on futures exchanges, which are regulated in the United States by the Commodities Futures Trading Commission (CFTC). Exchanges are subject to extensive regulation, and the FCMs who fill the role of matching buyers and sellers on these exchanges are also subject to minimum capital requirements and other regulations. The matching of buy and sell orders on the exchanges takes place through *floor brokers* acting by *open outcry* in the *trading pits,* which are small amphitheaters located in the large, open rooms in which the exchanges do business. Each contract has its own pit where traders in that contract congregate. If a customer calls his or her FCM to place an order to buy 20 S&P 500 March contracts at 600, this order will then be phoned to the FCM's order desk on the floor of the exchange, where it will be handed on a slip of paper to a runner who will carry it to the FCM's floor trader in the pit. The floor trader will then cry out that he or she has an order to buy 20 S&P 500 March contracts, and another floor trader who has an order to sell 20 such contracts will signal by hand a willingness to accept the offer. The buying and selling floor traders will note the trade in their books, and before the end of the day each floor trader will confirm the trade to the exchange record keepers.

The market in *forward contracts* operates much like the market in futures contracts, except that there is no central exchange for forwards as there is for futures. Instead, forwards are traded by direct negotiation, much as Thales did. By far the largest volume of forward contracts is traded in currency contracts, among banks. This interbank currency forward market is huge, trading hundreds of billions of dollars daily and operating 24 hours a day, 7 days a week, around the world, with no central exchange.

Traders in a New York bank, for example, might be given an order to enter a forward contract to buy 1 million deutsche marks for U.S.$700,000 next March. The traders will be watching a computer screen on which current trading is reflected to see if the price is realistic. If it is, they may then register their willingness to enter the contract by placing a bid on the computer network and by calling other bankers with whom they deal, or who they see via the screen may be willing to accept the bid, at that price or one close to it. The deal is then closed over the phone and later confirmed in writing, so that the one bank is obligated to produce the dollars, and the other bank obligated to produce the deutsche marks, on the specified date in March. No exchange guarantees that each bank counterparty will perform its obligations, but the bankers are sufficiently familiar with each others' credit that they are willing to rely on it to ensure that the obligations of the forward contract will be met. The contract entered in each case is subject to negotiation and modification by the two banks who are entering it, rather than being a standardized contract mandated by an exchange. However, in most cases the banks refer to standardized customary terms.

If the order to buy a forward deutsche mark contract is not filled during the New York trading day, presumably because the market has not been trading at the specified price, the bank's New York trading desk may at the end of its day pass the order on to the bank's trading desk in Hong Kong or Tokyo, which opens for business as the New York desk is preparing to close. If the order is not filled in Hong Kong by the time its trading desk closes, it will be passed on to the bank's London trading desk, which is open as Hong Kong is closing. If not filled in London, it will be passed back to New York when London closes and New York is again open. This market functions 24 hours a day, requiring a team approach to trading because of the obvious demands of human physiology. Avid foreign exchange traders, however, leave orders to be awakened by telephone if significant developments occur during their home-city night, and they keep trading screens running at home and office 24 hours a day.

Banks are of course regulated by the U.S. Comptroller of the Currency, and in some cases by the Federal Reserve Board and by state regulators. The CFTC does not regulate forwards, and has issued rules distinguishing futures from forwards. A contract is defined as a forward and not a future if it has individually tailored terms, is not subject to exchange-style offset, is not executed through an exchange clearinghouse or mark-to-market margining system, is entered into in conjunction with the parties' line of business, and is not marketed to the general public. Also, forwards provide parties with the ability to *require* physical delivery. While the forward market is therefore defined as a market in which contracts are custom-made and carried out among counterparties in that line of business, anyone can trade in the market by establishing an account at a bank or other currency forward dealer, much as an account is established with a futures commission merchant.

Currency forward contracts trade in a large and very liquid market. It is easy to place trades or to place a second trade canceling out the first. Other types of forward contracts may be as specialized as the needs of the parties entering them—a forward contract might be entered on olive presses, for example, just as

Thales did. Forwards can be completely customized, unlike exchange contracts, which are completely standardized, but the investor must find a suitable counterparty. The investor also bears the risk of the counterparty's default, and there is no FCM or exchange clearinghouse to guarantee performance. It may be harder to close out a forward position, since the counterparty may not be interested in closing out the contract before its expiration date, even at a market price. Although the contract can always be closed by mutual agreement, it is unlikely that both parties are going to be interested in closing the contract at the same time. However, as discussed in the section on swaps, dealers can simplify and manage these transaction costs and risks.

HOW OPTIONS WORK

There are two types of options: *puts* and *calls.* Either type can be bought or sold, so there are four distinctly different types of option investments. These four types, and some basic concepts regarding options, are reviewed in this section, which concludes with a summary table. People dealing in options often have to think twice to be sure they are clear on what they are doing. An option can consist of a right to buy an underlying asset (a call option) or a right to sell an underlying asset (a put option). Either type of option can itself be bought or sold. That is, one can buy a put or a call, or one can sell a put or a call.

In *buying a call,* an investor acquires the right, but not the obligation, to buy an underlying asset for a specified price during a specified period of time. For example, the investor who pays $3,000 to buy a "December 102 call option" on a $100,000 U.S. Treasury bond has the right, until December, to buy that bond at an *exercise price* (also called a *strike price*) of 102 ($102,000).

If the market price of U.S. Treasury bonds is now 101, the call option has no *intrinsic value,* and is said to be *out of the money,* because no one would exercise the call option to buy a Treasury bond for 102 when the bond could be purchased on the open market for 101. Nevertheless, the call option *sells* for $3,000 because of the possibility that the price of Treasury bonds may rise before December, when the option *expires.* This $3,000 price for an out-of-the-money option is called its *time value.*

If the price of Treasury bonds falls to 93, the price of the call option will fall, because it will take a bigger market price increase to give the call option any intrinsic value before it expires. That is, the price of Treasury bonds must rise from the market price of 93 to above the strike price of 102 before the bond will have any intrinsic value. Since this is a greater increase than that from a market price of 101 to 102, the probability is less that there will be any intrinsic value, and so the value of the option is much less when the market price is 93 than when the market price is 101.

If the price of Treasury bonds rises to 110, the call option will have an intrinsic value of $8,000 (the market price of 110 less the strike price of 102 equals 8). When an option has intrinsic value, it is said to be *in the money.* However, it will sell for more than $8,000 because there will still be an additional time value to the option. There is still a possibility that market price of Treasury bonds will rise further, above 110, before the call option expires in December.

By definition, the market price of an option equals its intrinsic value plus its time value. Sometimes, intrinsic value is zero. An option that is out of the money has no intrinsic value, so its only value is its time value, which depends on the probability that market price changes will move the option into the money before it expires. Time value depends on the evaluation in the marketplace of the probability that this will happen. An option that is in the money has both intrinsic value and time value.

In *selling a call*, the investor takes exactly the opposite side of the trade just described. Instead of paying $3,000 for the right to buy the Treasury bond for $102,000 during the option period, the investor receives $3,000 for undertaking the obligation to sell the Treasury bond for $102,000 during the option period. If the investor already owns a Treasury bond called for by the option contract, the investor has sold, or *written*, a *covered call.* If the investor doesn't own a Treasury bond (or a futures contract on such a bond, which is the same thing) the investor has sold an *uncovered call*, also referred to as a *naked call.* Unlike the buyer of the call, whose loss is limited to the $3,000 premium paid for the call, the seller of the call has unlimited liability, and will have to deliver the Treasury bond at the call price, whatever the cost to do so.

If a call is sold for 102 and the price rises to 110, the seller will lose $8,000 (less the $3,000 premium received), the equivalent of buying the bond at $110,000 and selling it for $102,000. Of course, if the seller of the call already owns a Treasury bond, he or she won't have to buy it on the open market, and will have made an $8,000 profit on the bond, offsetting the loss on the option. On the other hand, if the option expires without ever having any intrinsic value, the seller of the call can keep the $3,000 cost of the call as pure profit. Options may expire worthless, so this might seem like a good bet. However, it is like picking up dimes on the road in front of a bulldozer: One slip can be very costly.

In *buying a put,* an investor acquires the right, but not the obligation, to *sell* an underlying asset for a specified price during a specified period of time. For example, an investor who pays $3,000 to buy a "December 98 put option" on a $100,000 U.S. Treasury bond has the right, until December, to sell that bond at a *strike price,* or *exercise price* of 98 ($98,000). The buyer of a put is in effect placing a bet that the underlying asset will fall in value. If the price of the T-bond doesn't fall below the strike price, the investor simply loses the cost of the put. If it does fall below the strike price, the investor will receive a profit equal to the market price less the strike price and the cost of the put. If the party making this bet actually owns a $100,000 Treasury bond, the bet amounts to the purchase of insurance—an effective risk reduction strategy. That is, if the market price of Treasury bonds rises, investors can keep the profit they make on the Treasury bonds they own, though they will lose the premium they paid to buy the put. If the market price of Treasury bonds falls below the exercise price, their loss on the Treasury bonds they own will be offset by the profit on the put options they have purchased—less, of course, the premium they paid for buying the put option insurance.

In *selling a put,* an investor takes exactly the opposite side of that trade. The seller of the put receives $3,000, and is obliged to buy the bond for $98,000 during the time period of the put option. Of course, this obligation won't be called upon unless the price of the bond is less than 98. Otherwise the owner of the put will be able to get a higher price by selling the bond on the open market. But if the price of T-bonds plummets, the seller of the put will be forced to pay the difference between that price and the exercise price of the put, however great that may be.

The seller of an option is in effect the writer of an insurance policy—receiving a premium at the outset for taking an open-ended risk. The buyer of the option is the buyer of an insurance policy—paying a premium at the outset for the possibility of open-ended gain or a capped loss. The insurance can be bought or sold whether or not one owns the asset being insured. If one owns the asset being insured, and buys insurance, the transaction is a very conservative one, reducing risk at the price of the premium.

The first chart in figure 1.3 illustrates the value of a long call option at expiration. If the widget price is below the strike price of the option, the option expires worthless, and the holder loses the cost of the option. As the widget price rises above the strike price, the option gains value. The second chart in figure 1.3 illustrates the value of a long put option at expiration. If the widget price is above the strike price, the put option has no value. As the widget price falls below the strike price, the option gains value.

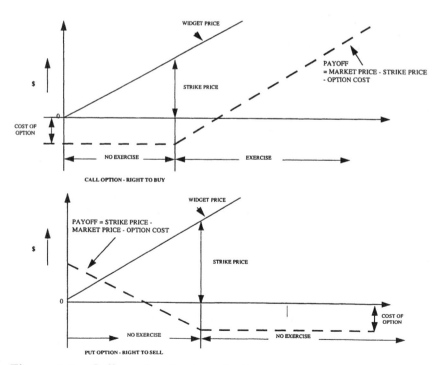

Figure 1.3 Calls and puts at expiration.

Summary Table

Put	Call
Intrinsic value = strike price – market price of asset (but not less than zero)	Intrinsic value = market price of asset – strike price (but not less than zero)

Market value of either a put or a call = intrinsic value + time value

(Intrinsic value can be calculated as above. Market price of the option is set by the market. The market price less any intrinsic value is the time value, or time premium, which depends on the time remaining before the option expires and also on the marketplace evaluation of the likelihood that intrinsic value will increase. The more *volatile* the price of the underlying asset, the greater the time value. Complex mathematical models, many based on the pioneering Black-Scholes model, attempt to determine the "fair value" of options based on formulas describing these relationships among options of varying expiration dates and strike prices.)

	Put	Call
Buy	Right to sell an asset Pay an option premium Maximum loss is the cost of option	Right to buy an asset Pay an option premium Maximum loss is the cost of option
Sell	Obligation to buy an asset Collect an option premium Maximum loss is the strike price less the premium received	Obligation to sell an asset Collect an option premium Maximum loss is unlimited

THE OPTIONS MARKET

Options are available on the stocks of larger corporations, on market indexes, on foreign and domestic government bonds and bills, on agricultural, industrial, and financial futures, and on foreign currencies. Options on stocks and stock indexes are traded on the stock exchanges; options on futures are traded on the futures exchanges. Stock options are generally sold in units equivalent to 100 shares of stock, while options on futures are usually for one futures contract. Most stock options and futures options are written for periods of a few months, although longer-term periods are available on the stocks of some large corporations and on stock and bond indexes. Customized options of all sorts are bought and sold away from the exchanges by many banks and dealers.

2

Swaps and
Structured Notes

FOREIGN CURRENCY SWAPS
AND INTEREST RATE SWAPS

Like options and futures, the idea underlying a swap is simple. It is the same idea that underlies any kind of trade or commerce. Party A has a product or commodity that party B needs, and vice versa. Both parties could theoretically produce the needed goods themselves, but for some reason or another not as cheaply. In other words, it is more efficient for both parties to specialize where they have an advantage, trading these goods for the other goods they need with producers who have a comparative advantage in that other market.

This type of comparative advantage is often very clear in international finance. Indeed, it is the basis for the currency swap, which allows a party receiving payments based on one currency to exchange these for payments based on another currency. For example, imagine a U.S. company that wishes to expand into France and wants to obtain financing denominated in French francs. The U.S. company probably has access to a good source of credit in the United States, where it may have special contacts and past experience with certain lenders, and where the lenders are confident of their ability to enforce the terms of the loan. The U.S. company might not be able to obtain quite as good a loan from a French bank. Now imagine a French company in the opposite position: that is, with a good source of credit in France but with the need for financing in the United States. Basically, the U.S. company has a comparative advantage in producing debt in the United States, and the French company has a comparative advantage in producing debt in France. Rather than attempting to "produce" both goods themselves, they are better off trading with each other. Figure 2.1 illustrates the details of the transaction. The first chart in figure 2.1 illustrates the first part of the swap. The U.S. company borrows from the U.S. bank and swaps this amount with the French company, which has borrowed from the French bank. The second chart in figure 2.1 indicates that as interest becomes due, the U.S. company pays the interest in French francs to the French company, which pays the French bank. At the same time, the French company pays the interest in U.S. dollars to the U.S. company, which pays the U.S. bank. So long as they are aware of each other, need a similar amount of money for a similar amount of time, and are both creditworthy, the currency swap will allow each to obtain a lower rate of interest than would be possible without the swap.

Currency swaps are a way of eliminating (or exploiting, depending on how you look at it) differences between international capital markets. Interest rate swaps can accomplish the same thing—eliminating barriers caused by different market access and regulatory structures.

The interest rate swap is very common, and it is quite similar to a currency swap. One form of basic interest rate swap allows a party who is receiving payments based on a fixed interest rate to exchange this stream of payments for a stream of payments based on a variable rate (often called a *floating* rate). The basic interest rate swap can be used to exploit comparative advantages between parties who are better at producing fixed or variable interest rate cash flows; and it also clearly illustrates how swaps can be used to hedge against risks, just like futures or options.

For example, a savings and loan association may have a very good source of fixed interest rate income: the mortgage payments

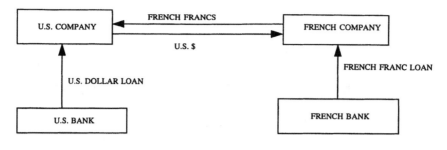

INITIAL CASH FLOWS

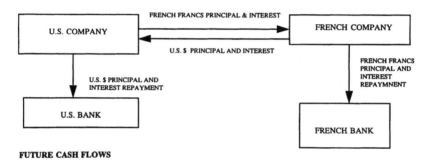

FUTURE CASH FLOWS

Figure 2.1   Currency swap.

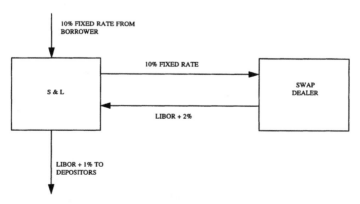

Figure 2.2   Interest rate swap.

from many homeowners to whom the S&L has made home loans. However, the S&L has floating rate liabilities. The S&L must pay its depositors interest on their deposits at current short-term rates. The S&L may receive a fixed rate from its home loan borrowers averaging 10 percent, but it may have to pay its depositors a variable rate, such as LIBOR + 1 percent. (LIBOR is the rate of interest offered by banks on deposits from other banks in the Eurocurrency markets.) If the variable rate rises above the fixed rate, the S&L will be paying more interest than it receives, and it will begin to lose money. If it can swap the mortgage payments for a variable rate greater than the variable rate it pays to its depositors (such as LIBOR + 2 percent) it will have a guaranteed stream of income. Its *spread* will be 1 percent, which is the difference between the interest it receives, at LIBOR + 2 percent, and the interest it pays, at LIBOR + 1 percent. This profit margin will remain constant whether the LIBOR rate itself rises or falls. The S&L has insulated its business from unpredictable fluctuations in interest rates, which could cause its profits to soar or plummet. Instead, by use of the swap, the S&L has guaranteed itself a steady profit on its business of gathering deposits from savers and making mortgage loans to homeowners. (See figure 2.2.)

Transactions such as this are commonplace today, and they allow the bank's lending department to concentrate on the business of lending. The swap allows the bank to focus the risks it is interested in taking as part of its business. The lending department's success will depend on its success in making loans and its ability to evaluate the credit of its borrowers, not its ability to predict how interest rates will change.

Unlike futures and options, swaps are not traded on exchanges, although some modern swaps, especially plain-vanilla interest and currency swaps, are extremely liquid and actively traded on an informal market among dealers. Other swaps remain highly customized contracts designed to meet the specific risk management or investment needs of sophisticated businesses and investors. Because of this, the changing role of the swap dealer has been very important to the evolution of the swap market in recent years.

Because someone must find and bring together two parties who have equal and opposite needs, there is always a niche for a broker to arrange even simple swaps. The more complex the swap, however, the more difficult it is to find a party with equal and opposite needs; in fact, it is often likely a single counterparty simply cannot be found to match many swap needs. The swap dealer, implementing principles of modern finance through the use of various derivative products, has solved this problem by transforming the role of the broker into that of a risk intermediary. In the process, the swap dealer has created a whole new repertoire of methods to control risk and exploit comparative advantages. This role emerged to meet the needs of businesses and investors in the development of the swap market.

Currency swaps predated interest rate swaps by several years. There are several claimants to the honor of arranging the first currency swap, but the general view is that currency swaps as we know them began to emerge in the late 1970s. These were matched transactions arranged between counterparties with equal and opposite needs. One of the parties might need payments in yen; another might need payments of the same amount in Swiss francs. The format for these early-period currency swaps was that of parallel loans. That is, each party entered into loan agreements with the opposite party in the amount of notional principal needed. A U.S. company might loan a Japanese company $100,000,000; the Japanese company might at the same time loan the U.S. company an equivalent amount of Japanese yen.

In some cases, these early transactions were arranged to circumvent some form of exchange control. Government regulations might forbid exchanging pesos for dollars but might not forbid lending pesos and borrowing dollars. The parallel loan mechanism for this sort of swap was justified, from the point of view of the company, by an extreme situation of comparative advantage. The economics of the transaction were impossible without it because of stringent governmental restrictions on the ability of borrowers and lenders to convert the foreign government's currency to other currencies needed in their business. The parallel loan market was not very large, and only a handful of bankers had the patience and tenacity to work on these transactions over the long lead times needed to bring them to fruition. There were probably not more than a handful of people worldwide working on these deals. They were complicated, took a long time to consummate, and needed a global network of clients, which was essential to identify counterparties with equal and opposite needs.

These deals were usually fully matched between counterparties—to a degree that would seem absurd in the market today. For example, long hours were spent discussing business-day conventions. If a currency swap had counterparties in Europe and the United States and included the Japanese yen, the banker had to ensure that payments to various parties falling due on business holidays were matched exactly, such that the intermediary bank was never at risk of making a payment before the receipt of the offsetting payment under the swap.

Over the span of 15 years, these practices have been transformed. The market has progressed from such minutiae as concern about intraday payment risk to a level where junior traders make commitments on $100 million transactions subject to documentation, which sometimes is not completed and signed for months.

After currency swaps had been present in the marketplace for several years, the first interest rate swap was arranged in the early 1980s. Like currency swaps, interest rate swaps in the early stages of the market were arranged on a fully matched basis by bank intermediaries between counterparties with equal and opposite needs. One of the parties might need fixed rate financing for $300 million but have access to a good source of floating rate financing; another might need floating rate financing for $300 million but have access to a good source of fixed rate financing.

The early interest rate swaps were almost all based on the U.S. dollar and had a common theme. European and Japanese banks of the highest credit standing discovered that they could borrow money at very favorable rates by issuing fixed rate debt in the Eurobond market. This was possible primarily because of the demand for such high-quality bank debt in that market and the small supply of such debt at that time. However, the banks needed large amounts of funds on a floating rate (LIBOR) basis to participate in making loans in the huge and rapidly growing syndicated loan markets, where the interest on most loans was calculated on floating rates. The main sources of floating rate funds that the banks could use were deposits and floating rate note issues. Both these sources generated funds at a cost to the banks equal to, or slightly above, LIBOR rates.

Across the Atlantic, in the United States, a different set of circumstances had developed. A number of corporate borrowers needed long-term, fixed rate financing and had used the fixed rate bond markets in the United States extensively. Because so much money was being raised by corporations in this way, leading to a large supply of this paper, investors were able to demand historically high interest rates relative to the interest rates offered on U.S. Treasury securities. This situation was most clearly evident in the case of utility companies that had large borrowing needs and quite appropriately wanted to borrow on a fixed rate basis to match the long-term, fixed rate nature of their cash flows. But the cost of financing at a fixed price was fairly high, while at the same time these utilities could borrow from banks on reasonable terms on a floating rate basis.

One bright person looked at this situation and arranged the following transaction. A certain AAA-rated European bank borrowed money on a fixed rate basis by issuing bonds in the European bond market where it had the greatest comparative advantage due to its presence and reputation in that market. At the same time, a U.S. utility borrowed on a floating basis from the U.S. bank where it had the greatest comparative advantage due to its presence and reputation. Then, through a financial intermediary, the European bank exchanged its fixed rate obligation for the floating rate obligation of the U.S. utility. In this way, the U.S. utility had the fixed rate loan it wanted, and the European bank had the floating rate loan that best matched its floating rate obligations to its depositors. Each party got its preferred form of financing at rates cheaper than existing alternatives. In other words, the banks had a comparative advantage in raising fixed rate money; the utilities had a comparative advantage in raising floating rate money. Swaps allowed these comparative advantages to be exploited to their mutual benefit, even across international boundaries.

In an efficient financial market, when this sort of arbitrage opportunity presents itself, it is quickly exploited. Once the first transaction is completed, more transactions follow, and the parties involved do not rest until the arbitrage opportunity is completely exhausted. Eventually, so many interest rate swaps were completed that, in the course of this boom, interest rate swaps overtook currency swaps in terms of volume and numbers of counterparties.

Sometime in the latter half of 1982, one of the intermediary banks that was a dominant force in the swap market decided to undertake a transaction that revolutionized the swap business. This bank decided that it was not necessary to have counterparties with equal and opposite needs in order to create a swap. The swap team at this bank observed that they could commit to one side of an interest rate swap transaction and then go looking for the other side subsequently. In the interim period, they would hedge their interest rate exposure by taking the appropriate long or short position in Treasury bond futures of the same duration. In fact, the bank did not even need to find a single counterparty, but could find several smaller counterparties with the opposite need that in total matched the size of the original counterparty. Alternatively, they could find a counterparty who needed the swap for a different duration and hedge the net exposure in the futures or forwards markets.

The next step in the evolution of the market was fairly easy. If swaps could be done without a counterparty with a matching transaction in hand, it really was not necessary to find a matching counterparty at all. Why not treat every swap on an individual basis, collect the swaps into a single portfolio in which many counterparties on different sides of different transactions would tend to some extent to cancel out each other's risk, and then compute the remaining net risk of the portfolio and enter a hedge transaction to eliminate it?

Even if individual swaps are not made on a matched basis, it is likely that in the aggregate they will offset each other substantially. Some customers will have swapped fixed for floating liability; others will have swapped floating for fixed. Once the swaps are collected into a portfolio, the dealer can compute whether more money is exposed to floating or to fixed risk and enter into separate futures or forward hedges to protect against the residual floating or fixed risk. The protection can be obtained by use of futures contracts on an exchange, a forward contract with another dealer, or even a swap transaction whereby one swap dealer exchanges the residual floating rate risk for the residual fixed rate risk of another swap dealer.

Once a number of institutions started doing this, the interest rate swap market became a trading market. Swap dealers traded swaps with other dealers directly as a way of minimizing the risk in their portfolios. Swaps became liquid contracts both for the dealers and the customers, who could easily meet their swap needs without the necessity of a counterparty, and could close these swap contracts by negotiating directly with the dealer rather than with a counterparty. By the middle of 1983, a number of intermediaries had active trading books in U.S. dollar interest swaps. Swaps books in DM, SwFr, ¥, and £ followed rapidly in the next 6 to 12 months.

SWAPTIONS, CAPS, AND FLOORS

A swap is merely a contract, and there is no reason it cannot be combined with other types of derivatives, just as your home mortgage contract contains various types of derivatives.

An option on a swap (or *swaption*) gives the party the right, but not the obligation, to enter into a swap at a later date. This is useful when a party expects to need a swap at a later date (should certain business eventualities develop) and finds the present price for such a swap appealing, but does not wish to commit to the swap until it is absolutely necessary.

A cap or a floor in a swap may be used to set an outer limit to the amount the floating rate side of a swap will be forced to pay. A *cap* is an upper limit; a *floor* is a lower limit. Since the upper limit provides an advantage to the party paying the interest and exposes the counterparty to a risk if the limit comes into effect, the party paying the interest must pay for the cap, like paying an option premium for the insurance that the cap provides. For example, the party paying floating rate interest under a swap might be required to pay LIBOR + 1 percent, capped at 10 percent; the party paying the floating rate interest will pay a price for the 10 percent cap. In contrast, a floor obligates the party to keep paying interest at the floor rate, even if the rate as otherwise calculated would be lower. The party agreeing to the floor is therefore paid for that obligation, like collecting an option premium for the insurance that the floor provides the counterparty.

A *collar* is a combination of a cap and a floor, placing both an upper and a lower limit on the rate. For example, for LIBOR + 1 percent, capped at 10 percent with a floor of 4 percent, the rate paid will be determined by LIBOR + 1 percent, except that it will never exceed 10 percent or fall below 4 percent. So long as LIBOR plus 1 percent equals between 4 and 10 percent, the holder of the collar receives that amount. However, if LIBOR plus 1 percent falls below 4 percent, the holder of the collar continues to receive 4 percent. Conversely, if it rises above 10 percent, the holder will receive no more than 10 percent. (See figure 2.3.) A *costless collar* is one in

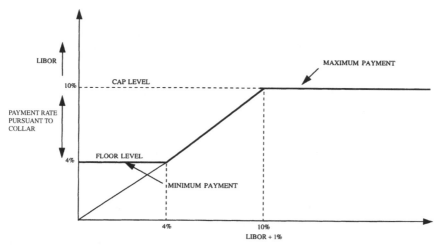

Figure 2.3   Floating rate interest payment with cap/floor collar.

which the amount that one pays to buy the cap is equal to the amount one receives for selling the floor. In all these cases it is theoretically possible that a counterparty could be found willing to accept exactly the terms and limits desired by another counterparty, but most of these more complicated swaps are possible only through a dealer who is managing a portfolio of swaps and options, and who accepts or hedges away any residual risk.

STRUCTURED NOTES

A structured note is nothing more than a normal note in which some part of the payment is based on a derivative. The first broad application of structured notes appeared in the form of dual-currency private placements in the Swiss market. The notes had coupons (interest payments) denominated in Swiss francs and a principal repayment in dollars. This dual-currency structure resulted in coupon rates somewhere between Swiss franc interest rates, which were very low, and U.S. dollar interest rates, which were quite high. The resulting high coupons were very attractive to Swiss retail investors who had perhaps viewed the world as very stable. They apparently did not expect the number of Swiss francs that could be purchased by U.S. dollars to decline too much, and therefore were not very concerned with the risk of loss of principal on redemption, at which point they would be repaid in U.S. dollars, which might buy fewer Swiss francs than those used to purchase the note originally. (Of course, if the U.S. dollar appreciated against the Swiss franc so that more Swiss francs could be purchased with the U.S. dollars received on redemption, the investor would have profited from the exchange rate fluctuation.) There were a number of such issues around 1984, followed by a spate of dual-currency yen/dollar bonds in the Japanese private placement market. The first chart in figure 2.4 below shows the payment stream for a 4 percent Swiss franc note. The second shows the payment stream for a 10 percent U.S. note. The third shows a note paying 8 percent interest payments in Swiss francs and principal repayment in dollars. A Swiss investor who buys the latter will receive higher interest payments than with the Swiss franc note, but if the value of the dollar relative to the Swiss franc falls, the repayment will be worth less than a repayment in Swiss francs.

In some respects, these dual-currency notes were the precursor to the development of the structured note market in the United

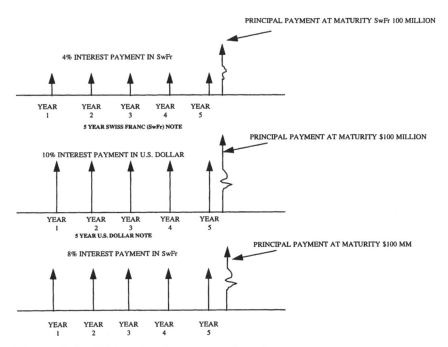

Figure 2.4   5-Year dual currency bond.

States starting about 1987. The structured notes market which dominated the news in the early 1990s originated with a number of multicurrency-linked securities. These securities were similar to the dual-currency placement described previously, but grew progressively more complicated. For example, so-called reverse currency-linked securities allowed an investor to benefit if a foreign currency fell in value. Currency-linked securities also began to appear with higher and higher levels of leverage.

Multicurrency-linked securities accomplish this by having a repayment at maturity that is based on two different currencies. As an example, a note sold for $100 million today might include terms under which the repayment will consist of an amount calculated as $200 million less ¥10 billion. If present exchange rates are 100 yen to the dollar, the yen are valued at $100 million, so that using today's exchange rates, the total repayment is calculated at $200 million less $100 million, or a net of $100 million. However, if the value of yen increases, the value of the dollar repayment decreases. If the value of yen increases 10 percent, the repayment amount will be calculated as $90 million. Leverage is added by increasing the amounts used in the formula. For example, the same original principal value of $100 million, based on today's exchange rates, could be achieved by basing repayment on $300 million − ¥20 billion. In this case, however, an increase in the value of yen will affect the repayment twice as much as in the original formula. A 10 percent rise in the value of yen will result in a repayment amount of $80 million. The securities are leveraged two to one. Figure 2.5 illustrates how this leverage works. If the exchange rate at expiration is the same as at purchase, both securities will pay the same amount. However, if the exchange rates are different, security II will be affected twice as much as security I, because it is leveraged 2 to 1.

For a while, these securities worked out nicely for investors in an environment of exchange rate stability in the European markets. However, near the end of 1993, the prevalent exchange rate mechanisms broke down, and most investors suffered losses which were magnified by the high levels of leverage incorporated within these notes. Around the same time, the yen/dollar exchange rate entered into a secular slide, with the dollar depreciating rapidly and continuously from around 140¥/$ to 85¥/$, which resulted in high losses on the numerous yen-based multicurrency structured notes.

	Purchase Price	Maturity	Coupon	Redemption
Security I	$100 MM	5 Years	5%	$200 Million-Yen 10 Billion
Security II	$100 MM	5 Years	7%	$300 Million-Yen 20 Billion

Spot exchange rate at purchase: 100 Yen/$

Note: In both cases redemption value equals purchase price if FX rate at Maturity equals FX rate at purchase.

FX Rate at Maturity	Redemption Value			
	Security I	Difference from Par	Security II	Difference from Par
110 Yen/$	$109.09	+$9.09	$118.18	+18.18
105 Yen/$	$104.76	+$4.76	$109.52	+9.52
100 Yen/$	$100.00	0	$100.00	0
95 Yen/$	$94.74	−$5.26	$89.47	−10.53
90 Yen/$	$88.89	−$11.00	$77.77	−22.23

Security II is leveraged twice as much compared to security I with respect to the YEN/$ exchange rate

Figure 2.5   Yen–dollar multicurrency-linked securities.

While all this was happening in the multicurrency structured notes market, the interest rate–based structured notes market was also enjoying an explosion of activity. This was fueled by a proliferation of exotic option-based structures, high embedded leverage, and most important, a rapidly falling interest rate. Most of these notes had embedded synthetic long positions with a high level of leverage. In a falling interest rate regime, this was a recipe for increasing profits. Until, of course, interest rates changed directions, and investors were suddenly faced with the ugly side of leverage, multiplying losses just as it multiplies profits.

During this period, all of the preceding concepts of multicurrency arbitrage, interest rate option–based structures, and high leverage were being presented as structured swaps to corporate treasurers who were more and more inclined to view their areas as profit centers. The most adventuresome corporate treasurers used these structured swaps and enjoyed the benefits of leverage and falling interest rates in the same fashion as those being used by investors, and similarly were confronted with the ugly side of leverage when interest rates turned around and began to rise.

The leveraged multicurrency-linked securities provide an interesting contrast with the use of derivatives by U.S. utilities and European banks. In the latter case, derivatives were used to take advantage of very real arbitrage opportunities involving little if any risk, and which benefited all parties—lower interest rates for both the utilities and the banks and the fixed rate financing the U.S. utilities wanted, combined with the floating rate financing European banks preferred. This arbitrage opportunity was enthusiastically exploited until the favorable interest rate differentials that gave rise to it no longer existed. In the case of the leveraged currency-linked securities, however, there was high risk, which was associated with high rewards so long as the market was moving favorably, but which was associated with equally high losses when market movements became unfavorable.

SUMMARY

The short history of currency and interest rate derivatives touches only a few of the highlights of this period and only certain segments of the market. A comprehensive account encompassing all the myriad products and applications would be an entire book in itself. However, we've covered a few important themes.

First, we have learned that swaps are at the heart of modern finance. Their highly customized use to solve particular business and investment problems is possible through swap dealers who can create these sophisticated tools, price them, and manage the risk of an entire portfolio of swaps far more efficiently than most institutional or individual users could. It is extremely difficult for individuals or most institutions to have the wherewithal to manage large, diverse portfolios.

Second, swaps can be used for many different purposes. They can be used to hedge risk, to exploit comparative advantages, or to make investments in the most efficient way. Swaps can also be combined with other derivative tools. Swaps can contain embedded options, caps, and floors. Many of the examples of hedging business risks and of using derivatives to make investments, described in later chapters, are possible only through swaps.

Third, structured financing accomplishes two things. First of all, it may allow a corporation to achieve a more favorable rate of financing. Even more important, it allows an issuer to design a product that is better tailored to the investor's need. In our experience, over 90 percent of the time, the issuer will fully hedge the variability of the payment formula. If payment is connected to a foreign currency, the issuer will enter into a swap at the time of issuance, which hedges away this risk, so that as far as the issuer is concerned, the issuer gets a simple fixed or floating rate obligation. In the early days, the issuer might still have gotten a savings of around 50 basis points, but as these methods became more common, the savings declined to around 15 to 20 basis points. Of course, in the 5 or 10 percent of transactions where the company does not hedge out all its exposure, the company may experience even greater interest rate savings, but at the cost of taking a currency risk, which may ultimately prove more costly than a simple fixed or floating rate issuance. The widespread use of structured financing has therefore resulted in a wide range of products that allow investors new ways to make their investments or to hedge their risks.

3

Mortgage "Derivatives"

COLLATERALIZED MORTGAGE OBLIGATIONS

Your home mortgage is part of the largest sector of the world's debt market: $3.5 trillion in 1990. Shortly after making the loan to you and obtaining the mortgage on your home, the bank making the loan probably paid a small premium to a government-sponsored federal agency, such as Fannie Mae (Federal National Mortgage Association, or FNMA), which then issued insurance that will pay the owner of the mortgage in the event you default. Once this insurance has been obtained, the bank that originated the mortgage very likely sold it, agreeing to continue to service the mortgage for its new owner by collecting payments from you, dealing with any questions you may have about the loan, enforcing the remedies under the mortgage by foreclosing on the house in case of defaults, and collecting any money that you may owe. The buyer of your mortgage, now backed by the credit of these federal government–sponsored agencies and serviced by the originating bank, has a high-quality financial asset, particularly when combined into a portfolio of many such mortgages.

In fact, your mortgage may then have been pooled with many other home mortgages into a bundle of assets, which were sold again to purchasers of securities, entitling the holders of those securities to receive the payments of principal and interest made by the individual homeowners on each of the mortgages.

Payments of principal and interest by homeowners on the individual mortgages underlying the security are often not passed through pro rata to the security holders. Rather than issuing one class of securities, each of which entitles the holder to a pro rata share of the payments, many different types of securities may be issued, all of which together add up to the whole of the rights to the payments on the underlying mortgages. For example, one class of security may be entitled to only principal payments made by the homeowners (a *principal-only strip*), while another may be entitled only to interest payments made by the homeowners (an *interest-only strip*); together, these add up to all the payments made by the homeowner, but some of the payments go to one class of security holders, some of the payments to another class, depending on whether the payments are principal or interest. There are many other variations in the division of rights to payments by the homeowner, and all of these securities are referred to as *mortgage derivatives*, since they are "derived" from the underlying mortgages through financial engineering. The right to these payments are cut up, "stripped," and recombined in a variety of ways. In this way, the rights to the payments on a package of home mortgages can be specifically tailored to an investor's risk and reward preferences, and entirely new instruments can be created from very traditional mortgage investments.

Today, mortgage-backed securities (MBSs) constitute a huge market—which is not surprising, considering that the mortgage market is in itself the largest sector of the debt market. Until the early 1980s, Wall Street had little role in this market. This has radically changed with the development of collateralized mortgage obligations (CMOs), the securitization of the mortgage market, and the slicing of mortgage pools into derivative securities through financial engineering.

Even before these derivative products emerged, banks repackaged their mortgages and sold them on the secondary market. Your mortgage may have been combined with hundreds of similar mortgages to constitute a pool of mortgages worth hundreds of millions of dollars. Interests in this pool were then sold as mortgage-backed securities (MBS) or pass-through securities, providing each investor with a fractional undivided interest in the pool of mortgage loans. You pay your mortgage interest and principal to the bank, and the bank may then forward the payment to the originator or trustee of the MBS, which redistributes this money to the different shareholders of the MBS.

In this way, an investor can purchase a small interest in a large pool of mortgages, thereby diversifying the risks that come from a single mortgage or a small number of mortgages. Mortgages are subject to two important risks: the risk of default and the risk of prepayment. Simple *mortgage pass-throughs* manage only the first risk, through diversification. The second arises from the prepayment option embedded in the mortgage, which allows the borrower to repay the loan in full at any time. CMOs were created to address the more complex problems created by this seemingly innocuous provision.

The default risk can vary widely and somewhat unpredictably from loan to loan. It is the risk the borrower will fail to make his or her payments, forcing the bank to repossess the property. A local presence by a local bank, thrift, or S&L is needed to evaluate the likelihood of default and the loss that may occur in repossessing and reselling the property requires. The bank that gave you your home mortgage may then purchase mortgage insurance from one of several different government-sponsored federal insurance agencies, such as FNMA. This loan can then be pooled with other loans to greatly reduce the risk of default on the whole diversified portfolio of loans. The bank that originally issued the loans will continue to collect the interest and principal payments on the loans and forward them to the pool's administrator, which in turn forwards them to the investors in the pool's securities. Should foreclosure be necessary, the servicing bank handles the foreclosure and sale, sending the proceeds on to the investors, along with any payments by the federal agency that are required to make up any deficit. The resulting pool of mortgages represents a highly diversified investment guaranteed by a federally sponsored agency.

But this kind of diversification does not address the problems caused by the prepayment option. This risk is really a kind of interest rate risk. Interest rate risk exists with the purchase of any kind of fixed rate bond. If interest rates increase beyond the rate paid on your bond, your bond will be paying less than the market rate of interest, so if you need to sell the bond you will get less than its face value. Interest rate risk is aggravated in mortgage-backed securities because home mortgages usually include an *embedded option* allowing the mortgagee to *prepay* the principal without any penalty. If you move to a new house you will probably sell your house and pay off the balance of the old mortgage with the proceeds from the sale. If interest rates come down, you may decide to refinance your home at a lower rate, and this will also result in your paying off the balance of the old mortgage. In either case, you will be able to pay off the old mortgage entirely without any penalty.

These prepayments are not random in time—if they were, their risk could easily be mitigated through the diversification of large mortgage pools. In fact, prepayments occur most often when the borrower refinances the loan, and refinancing occurs most often when interest rates fall. Prepayments due to home sales may also become more common in the environment of falling interest rates.

The risk to the investor is therefore not random, nor is it easily predictable or manageable. When interest rates fall, large numbers of homeowners may refinance. (This is called *contraction risk.*) The investor gets his or her cash back, but at the worst possible time. The low interest rates that drove the homeowners to refinance will also make it impossible for the investor to reinvest his or her cash at the same rate of return being received before the prepayment. If interest rates increase, homeowners have a greater incentive to hold on to their lower-interest loans, and prepayments will actually decrease. This is called *extension risk,* since under such circumstances the investor would be delighted to get his or her cash back and be able to reinvest it at the higher interest rates then prevailing.

This was the big problem in selling mortgage-backed securities before the 1980s and the reason that many mortgages remained the property of banks and savings and loans until that time. Investors were not interested in bonds with an unpredictable maturity, and homeowners were not willing to give up the prepayment option in their mortgages or to pay a sufficient prepayment penalty to compensate the investor for the early return of his or her money at a time when the investor couldn't get the same interest rate elsewhere. Accordingly, banks had to keep their mortgages and the prepayment risk that went along with them. Several developments made these securities more marketable.

The first had nothing to do with derivatives. In 1981, with thrifts on the verge of collapse, Congress granted a tax break to them which created an incentive for thrifts to sell their loan portfolios. Subsidized by the tax break, thrifts could sell mortgages to investors at substantial discounts, and these discounts were sufficient to induce investors to accept the risks inherent in the unpredictable maturity. This made it feasible for large pools of mortgage-backed securities to be created on Wall Street and marketed to investors.

Second, stimulated by this boom in sales of mortgage-backed securities, Wall Street brokers and lawyers invented ways to carve up the mortgage-backed securities so as to make them more predictable to some investors: the CMO, which was later legislated into the real estate mortgage investment conduit (REMIC). (See figure 3.1.)

In a CMO a special entity is created to receive all the mortgage payments, and then issues securities which, rather than giving the investor a simple pro rata fraction of the payments received, provides several different types of payments defined by different formulas representing one slice, or *tranche*, of the payments received. As an example, the tranche purchased by one investor might be the right to receive a portion of every interest payment (an interest-only strip, called an IO). Another investor's tranche might be the right to receive a portion of every principal payment (a principal-only strip, called a PO). So every month when you make a payment on your mortgage, the REMIC sends that part of your payment representing interest to the investor who bought the IO tranche, and that part of your payment representing principal paydown goes to the investor who bought the PO tranche. If you prepay your mortgage because you have sold or refinanced your house, the owner of the principal-only PO tranche gets a large payment, following which the owner of the interest-only or IO tranche will get no payments at all, since you will no longer be paying any interest.

This type of division does not actually eliminate the uncertainty caused by the prepayment option—it simply redistributes the risk by creating two different securities that react differently to this prepayment risk. If prepayments occur rapidly, the IO loses

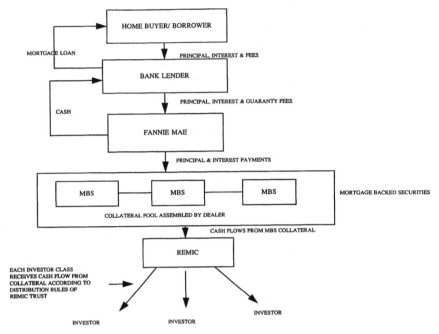

Figure 3.1   REMIC structure.

value quickly as interest payments are cut off. If prepayments occur very slowly, the PO loses value quickly as the prospect of payment moves further and further into the future. To truly limit the uncertainty, at least for certain classes of investors, a CMO needs to divide the tranches temporally. For example, Class A could be entitled to first-priority distributions every year equal to 12 percent of the amount of Class A tranches originally issued, the first 10 percent of the amount of Class A then outstanding being credited to interest, the balance to principal. These payments would be made from whatever source the CMO received funds from the mortgage payments, whether interest or principal. Class A shares would be a very predictable investment, receiving a level payment credited increasingly to principal until Class A investors were repaid in full. The other classes would bear all the prepayment risk, divided among them under whichever formulas produced the most marketable securities. Although the maturity of each class is still not exactly predictable, the original risk of prepayment has been effectively redistributed among the classes. The prepayment risk is now effectively eliminated for Class A, and the risk is correspondingly increased for the other classes.

Today, most CMOs have a large number of tranches, each geared to a specific customer's needs. In 1982, one of the earliest CMOs was issued for $50 million: It had two tranches. In 1983, there were eight CMO issues, with a dollar volume of $4,748 million, and an average of 6.6 tranches. In 1992, there were approximately 375 CMOs issued for *$188,458 million,* with an average of 17.7 tranches.

A particular class, or tranche, of a CMO can also be designed to imitate the performance of other securities and bonds. For example, an institutional investor may want a security with payments of interest for only seven years, followed by complete repayment of all principal at the end of the seventh year. Although it might be hard to find a pool of seven-year home mortgages, a CMO tranche can be designed with exactly these features. The inventiveness of financial engineers has not been limited to creating such simple instruments but has created entirely new products as well—pleasing a wide variety of customers in the process.

Unfortunately, the difficulty of predicting the timing of prepayments and of predicting interest rate fluctuations remains as great as ever. Some investor must bear the risk, so mortgage derivatives have merely provided investors with the means to pick and choose how much of that risk an investor wishes to take and to judge whether the price being offered is sufficiently attractive to offset the risk. In 1994, these risks came home with a vengeance when interest rates unexpectedly soared, reducing the value of PO strips and other tranches whose revenues depended on early payment. The resulting losses have at least temporarily greatly inhibited the salability of CMOs. New issues of CMOs have recently dropped from a rate of $300 billion a year to less than 10 percent of that amount. In fact, investors have become so gun-shy about taking any of these subdivided risks that the value of the parts of a mortgage fell below the value of the whole mortgage, so that it became worthwhile for some financial engineers to recombine the parts into securities that have the same characteristics as the whole mortgage.

SUMMARY OF CMOS

For the sake of understanding financially engineered derivatives, four important aspects of CMOs should be noted. First, they have proven immensely useful. Through this creative design, investors across the world can participate in a market that was previously limited to local banks. Cash-rich banks or investors in one area can purchase the loans of cash-poor institutions in another, allowing the latter to clear their mortgage portfolios and make new loans. Many types of derivatives offer the potential for similar benefits.

Second, part of the reason CMOs are so complicated is because the seemingly simple mortgage is itself deceptively complicated. The apparently inoffensive prepayment option in fact turns a mortgage into an instrument whose rate of return over time is very difficult to predict. As is the case with many derivatives, the CMO is simply a way of managing, or repackaging, the risk that is already present in the underlying mortgage.

Third, these derivatives do not eliminate the underlying risk, nor do they create a new type of risk; they simply redistribute the existing risk. In a simple CMO which is divided into tranches with different maturities, the prepayment risk is reduced in some tranches, but that risk increases correspondingly in other tranches.

Finally, these derivatives redistribute the underlying risk in accord with the needs of particular investors, and therefore may lead to a financial derivative that seems to be worlds apart from the underlying investment. For example, the rise of CMOs was also driven by an increased demand for fixed rate bonds, which some CMO tranches replicated. CMO tranches can also be designed to be used as a hedge for other risks. An IO or PO purchase could serve as a hedge for other bonds or investments that react in opposite ways to fluctuations in interest rates. Of course, not everyone wants to hedge, and the marketability of CMOs, like other derivatives, also depends on investors who are willing to take the risk if there is sufficient chance of gain.

The interrelation of these factors can lead to very complex instruments that *seem* to bear little relation to the underlying risk. For example, other common CMO tranches are the floater, inverse floater, and superfloater. A floating rate security, where the interest rate varies according to an index rate such as LIBOR, can be created out of a fixed rate security, provided there is someone who wants to purchase a security whose rate floats in the direction opposite to the same index. A *floater* payment will decrease as the index interest rates fall, and it will increase as they rise—the *inverse floater* does the opposite. The inverse floater is therefore a

LIBOR	LIBOR Floater at LIBOR	Inverse Floater at 14%—LIBOR Minimum: 0%	Superfloater 2 x LIBOR—6% Minimum: 0%
3%	3%	11%	0%
4%	4%	10%	2%
5%	5%	9%	4%
6%	6%	8%	6%
7%	7%	7%	8%
8%	8%	6%	10%
9%	9%	5%	12%
14%	14%	0%	22%
16%	16%	0%	26%

Figure 3.2   Floater, inverse floater, superfloater.

hedge against falling interest rates. A *superfloater* is a floater whose payments vary as a multiple of the index: If LIBOR rises 1 percent, the superfloater rises 2 percent; if LIBOR falls 1 percent, the superfloater falls 2 percent. Like a floater, issuance of a superfloater requires issuance of an inverse superfloater to balance out the effects within the portfolio of mortgages. Either a floater or superfloater could itself be sold as a hedge for another investment whose return varies inversely to that of the purchased hedge. (See figure 3.2.)

A regular or inverse superfloater may seem to be an exotic and potentially dangerous tool—for example, it was one of the many exotic and not-so-exotic investments used by Orange County. It also seems to bear little relationship to a modest suburban home in the Midwest. However, it is very directly affected by massive prepayments or foreclosures of such houses. It may serve as a hedge that allows a business to invest more freely in some new operation, or it may be bought by an investor hoping the reward is more than sufficient to compensate the risk.

4

Leverage

INTRODUCTION

Aristotle's story of Thales' "olive-press forwards" demonstrates "a principle of general application"—the principle of leverage. A small deposit controlled the use of an expensive olive press and produced revenues many times the size of the deposit. Thales was able to set up his monopoly by using leverage to rent many more olive presses than he could otherwise afford.

The examples in this section demonstrate some modern applications of this ancient principle of leverage. Leverage is perhaps the most important concept of finance and the key to understanding the very high returns, and risks, which are made possible or avoidable depending on how derivatives are used. It is a powerful tool. Leverage permitted Hillary Clinton to earn 10,000 percent profits in the cattle futures markets. The London merchant banking house of Baring Brothers, which had survived for centuries, was bankrupted by leverage in little over a month. Leverage is also essential to the vast majority of families in this country who participate in the American Dream of home ownership.

LEVERAGING YOUR HOUSE PURCHASE

We have already mentioned that your home mortgage contains a prepayment option. If you have a home mortgage, you not only have an option derivative, you are also using the most ancient and powerful financial tool known to humanity—leverage. Use of leverage in buying a house is very simple. You simply borrow part of the purchase price from a bank or other financial institution, undertaking the obligation to repay it with interest.

This decision to borrow part of the purchase price, rather than paying cash, profoundly affects the risk and return you can expect on your cash invested in the house. If you borrow 80 percent of the purchase price from the bank, you have five times the risk, and five times the potential return, on your cash investment than if you paid all cash for the house. Here is how it works.

If you pay $100,000 cash for a house, your percentage profit or loss on your investment will be exactly the same as the percentage increase or decrease in the market value of the house at the time you sell it. Figure 4.1 illustrates the point. You will lose 40 percent of your investment if the market value of the house falls to $60,000, or gain a 40 percent return on your investment if the market value of the house rises to $140,000.

Since the cash investment when leverage is used equals only one-fifth of the cash investment when leverage is not used, the percentage return on the leveraged investment is five times the percentage return on the unleveraged investment. (*Note:* Interest

Market Value	Original Cost	Profit or Loss	Percentage Profit or Loss
$ 60,000	$100,000	$−40,000	−40%
$ 80,000	$100,000	$−20,000	−20%
$ 90,000	$100,000	$−10,000	−10%
$100,000	$100,000	$ 0	0%
$110,000	$100,000	$ 10,000	10%
$120,000	$100,000	$ 20,000	20%
$140,000	$100,000	$ 40,000	40%
$400,000	$100,000	$300,000	300%

Figure 4.1 Home purchase, no leverage.

cost of borrowing is disregarded in this example. It would make the leveraged investment somewhat less attractive the longer the investment is held.)

Therefore, if you pay only $20,000 down on a $100,000 house, borrowing the rest, your gain or loss on your cash investment will be five times the percentage change in the market value of the house. Figure 4.2 shows the percentage gain or loss on a $20,000 down payment for a $100,000 house. Note that the market value, the cost of the house, and the dollar profit or loss are all the same in figures 4.1 and 4.2—but the percentage gain or loss on the $20,000 investment (figure 4.2) is exactly five times the percentage gain or loss on a house purchased for cash (see figure 4.3). A decline of 20 percent in the value of the house can destroy your whole investment. Worse, any decline greater than 20 percent may result in having to reimburse the bank for its losses. (This depends on the type of loan you have. When a house is sold in foreclosure at a loss greater than the cash down payment, the bank lender may ask the homeowner for reimbursement of its loss if the loan is *with recourse* to the borrower's other assets. However, the bank must bear the loss itself, and not ask the homeowner for reimbursement if the loan is *nonrecourse.* The difference between recourse and nonrecourse depends on the documentation of the loan. Some states, including California, require all loans made to purchase a home be nonrecourse.)

There's also an upside. If the price of a house goes up, the return on the leveraged investment is also five times higher than

Market Value	Original Cost	Investment	Profit or Loss	Percentage Profit or Loss
$ 60,000	$100,000	$20,000	$-40,000	-200%
$ 80,000	$100,000	$20,000	$-20,000	-100%
$ 90,000	$100,000	$20,000	$-10,000	-50%
$100,000	$100,000	$20,000	$ 0	0%
$110,000	$100,000	$20,000	$ 10,000	50%
$120,000	$100,000	$20,000	$ 20,000	100%
$140,000	$100,000	$20,000	$ 40,000	200%
$400,000	$100,000	$20,000	$300,000	1500%

Figure 4.2 Home purchase with leverage.

the nonleveraged investment. If the value of the house goes up from $100,000 to $140,000, you will make 200 percent on your investment rather than 40 percent.

To sum up, there are three important points to this example. First, without leverage, most Americans would not be able to own their own home. Most homeowners probably consider a mortgage to be merely a convenience, not an opportunity for leveraged speculation. Nevertheless, it should now be clear that the bread and butter of American investment depends upon leverage and includes an option (the option to refinance, discussed in chapter 3)—the same financial devices that allow the most aggressive investor to win or lose a fortune on the market. Furthermore, banks themselves are highly leveraged institutions. They depend on leverage to lend homeowners the money in the first place, and they use derivatives to repackage and sell their interests in the mortgages to investors across the world.

Second, the use of leverage (and the option) are not free. Interest must be paid on the home loan, along with numerous other fees and insurance. The additional protection afforded by nonrecourse loans, even if mandated by state laws, and the convenience of the embedded prepayment option are also not without cost.

Finally—and this point is critical—leverage adds risk. A small decline in the value of the house can wipe out the value of the cash invested for the down payment, and a larger decline can result in

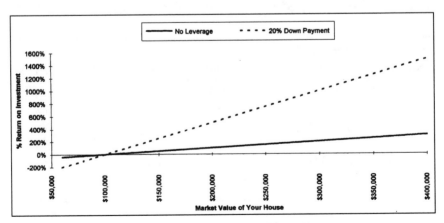

Figure 4.3   Leveraging your house purchase.

a loss of some of the borrowed money, a loss that must be borne by either the bank or the homeowner.

HILLARY CLINTON'S LEVERAGE

The power of leverage was recently publicized by Hillary Clinton's cattle futures market success—she turned $1,000 into $100,000 in about nine months. These gains not only required an incredible amount of "luck," but also an incredible amount of leverage. It is not our purpose to inquire how the trading decisions were made, but only to demonstrate that high leverage was an essential ingredient in the profits.

The price of cattle doubled between late 1977 and early 1979, moving from 40¢ a pound to 80¢ a pound. There had never been a price move like it before, nor has there been one since. Historically, this 40¢ increase in cattle prices was unique.

An investor smart enough to buy cattle at the very bottom for 40¢ a pound and sell at the very top for 80¢ a pound would have doubled his or her money—not a bad yearly return.

Hillary Clinton started trading cattle in October of 1978, well after this historic move was under way, when the price of cattle was already well over 50¢ a pound. She stopped trading in July of 1979, after the price had peaked and was plummeting back to under 60¢ a pound. Had she simply been buying and selling cattle for cash, she could not have doubled her money.

But she was not buying and selling cattle for cash, she was trading cattle futures, a derivative based on the price of cattle at a future date. And according to newspaper reports, she did not just double her money; she turned $1,000 into $100,000, multiplying her money 100 times—well over a 10,000 percent return. There is only one way this was possible: huge amounts of leverage.

A standard cattle futures contract is an obligation to buy or sell 40,000 pounds of cattle at a set date in the future. At 40¢ a pound, this is $16,000 worth of cattle. The 40,000 pounds of cattle is called the *notional amount* of cattle controlled by the contract, and $16,000 is the price to be paid for it in cash. If you buy a contract at this price and at the delivery date the price has increased to 42¢ a pound, the cattle will be worth $16,800—you have made $800. If you were the person who sold this contract, you have lost $800.

This is the obligation; but a futures contract is a contract to buy or sell in the future, and the investor is only required by futures exchange rules to deposit a percentage of the value of the contract with the broker (the *margin*). In this case, it would probably be around 7.5 percent, or about $1,200.

This is quite a small deposit—standing alone, it represents 13-to-1 leverage. An investor holding one futures contract for the entire, historic 40¢ increase in the price of cattle would have made 40¢ a pound times the 40,000 pounds covered by the contract, for a total of $16,000. However, the futures investor who has only $1,200 on margin does not just double his or her money. The futures investor will earn the same $16,000 as the unleveraged investor, with only a $1,200 deposit—a 1,333 percent profit.

As in the case of the house purchase, the leverage is not free. The full economic risk of loss is assumed by the investor, who is personally obligated on the entire contract (unlike the homeowner with a nonrecourse loan, whose loss will be limited to his or her investment). If the price of cattle falls 20¢ a pound, the loss on the position is $8,000 (20¢ times 40,000 pounds), and the investor must pay this amount to his broker, who forwards it through the exchange clearinghouse to those on the other side of the trade, just as the investor collects the profit through the exchange clearinghouse if the price of cattle goes up. Unlike a mortgage purchase, however, no interest is charged on the leverage. No money is borrowed; the $1,200 is just a deposit against the investor's contractual obligations.

The crux of the public focus on Hillary Clinton's trading is not that she succeeded within the rules just described; it is that she did even better than these rules allow by using more leverage than they permitted. In her first trade, on October 11, 1978, she made a $5,300 profit in one day on her $1,000 deposit. The *Wall Street Journal* reports that under exchange rules a $12,000 deposit would have been required to support the 10 futures contracts controlling the 400,000 pounds of cattle (worth $160,000) that were needed to make that profit. If Mrs. Clinton was personally obligated on the contracts, she was at risk for the full $160,000. Her broker simply may have extended more credit to her than exchange rules permitted.

If so, her broker permitted her to use leverage of 160 to 1, since a $1,000 deposit supported her commitment to buy $160,000 of cattle—exchange rules permitted leverage of only 13 to 1. Even 13 to 1, of course, is very high leverage. In a home purchase, the normal leverage is 5 to 1, so that a $32,000 deposit would be required to buy a $160,000 house, whereas Mrs. Clinton contracted to buy $160,000 worth of cattle with a $1,000 deposit.

The point here is the power of leverage. Without leverage, a doubling of the price of cattle turns $1,000 into $2,000. With the 13 to 1 leverage permitted by the exchange, the same move turns $1,000 into $13,000. With leverage at times reaching 160 to 1, Hillary Clinton's account grew from $1,000 to $100,000 in less than a year.

Part 2

DERIVATIVES IN ACTION

INTRODUCTION

Having reviewed the all-important principle of leverage, and the basic types of derivatives—futures and forwards, options, swaps, and financially engineered products—we will now examine their applications. After an overview of the four general uses of derivatives, which can of course be combined in various forms, we will discuss some applications in more detail, including the use of derivatives in hedging a stock portfolio, in hedging various business risks, and in making unleveraged investments. Many of the discussions focus on the use of publicly traded futures or options contracts, since these are available to all investors and businesspeople. If there is not a publicly traded contract that meets a specific need, however, private contracts can be arranged through derivatives dealers that can have similar characteristics as publicly available options or futures, and indeed can also have many other customized features. Depending on the situation, dealers will write these private contracts at competitive prices for transactions as small as the low seven figures. For smaller transactions, and many larger transactions, suitable alternatives are often available in the public markets, though perhaps not as exactly matched to individual needs.

5

Overview of Modern Derivatives Uses

USES OF DERIVATIVES

There are many kinds of derivatives, with innumerable uses, but their uses can be grouped into four general categories. A user of derivatives can (1) invest as a convenient, unleveraged substitute for the underlying asset, without undertaking any greater risk than that inherent in the underlying asset, (2) invest with the use of leverage, increasing risk and reward from that of the underlying asset in proportion to the leverage used, and therefore making any investment more speculative, (3) reduce risk by hedging, and (4) invest in a financially engineered asset which may bear little resemblance to the underlying asset, index, or combination of assets and indexes on which it is based, and which may be more suitable for the needs of a particular investor than any of the underlying assets.

DERIVATIVES AS AN UNLEVERAGED INVESTMENT: A PROXY FOR THE UNDERLYING ASSET

Conservative investment managers, such as those responsible for pension funds and university endowments, often use derivatives as a substitute for the underlying investment, without taking any greater risks or seeking any greater rewards than those inherent in the underlying investment. For example, buying stock index futures is no more nor less risky than investing in the stock market if the futures are bought without the use of leverage. Suppose a pension manager has just received a $100 million cash contribution from the company sponsoring the pension fund. The pension manager intends to invest the money in common stocks, but when the money comes in, the manager may not necessarily have a long list of stocks ready to buy that day. However, since the fund guidelines specify investment of a certain percentage of the fund assets in common stocks, the manager does not want to leave the money in cash and risk that the market may rise while taking the time to carefully select those particular stocks that may outperform the market. The manager wants to be "in the market" immediately, but doesn't want to go out and buy a group of stocks without sufficient analysis. Therefore, the manager buys stock index futures with a face amount of $100 million as a proxy for a well-diversified portfolio.

This purchase does not require the entire $100 million. Rather, it may require that only $5 million be deposited as margin with the broker, who may credit the fund with interest on this amount. The remaining $95,000,000 can be left in some other form of short-term cash investment where it also earns interest. Then, as the manager studies the markets and picks just the right time to buy particular stocks, he or she can buy the stocks and sell an equal face amount of the index futures at that time. Through this procedure, $100 million is invested in stocks at all times. More important, at no time is the portfolio leveraged. In fact, this particular use of index futures is no more risky than buying the individual stocks. The only difference is that instead of receiving dividends on $100 million worth of stocks from the outset, interest is received on the $95 million of cash deposits. The purchase of index futures is a cost-effective way to achieve the diversity of a large portfolio without the need to make hasty investment decisions in individual stocks.

DERIVATIVES FOR LEVERAGED INVESTING

The portfolio manager who buys $100 million in stock index futures and deposits $5 million in the margin account to cover obligations under the futures contracts is making an unleveraged investment only so long as he or she keeps another $95 million in either the margin account or in some other cash account earmarked for this investment. If the manager starts using the $95 million for other purposes, or doesn't have another $95 million, then to that extent the investment in stock index futures becomes a leveraged investment, since the manager has not reserved for the investment its full $100 million face value, either in the margin account or other reserves that can be transferred in part or whole into the margin account if the value of the stock index futures begins to fall. Figure 5.1 illustrates how an investment in stock index–based futures can be made on a leveraged or unleveraged basis. In strategy II, futures with a notional amount equal to $100 million are purchased on margin for $5 million, but the balance is held in cash. The portfolio will have the same risk and return as strategy I, in which $100 million worth of stock is purchased. In strategy III, the futures are purchased using the margin deposit alone, and no cash reserves are set aside. This 20-to-1 leverage leads to losses and gains that are 20 times greater.

		Investment	Leverage
Strategy I:	Buy basket of shares for cash	$100M	1:1
Strategy II:	Buy stock index futures & hold cash	Margin $5M+ cash $95M	1:1
Strategy III:	Buy stock index futures only	Margin $5M	20:1

	% Return on Investment	
	Market + 5%	**Market − 5%**
Gain/Loss	+$5M	−$5M
Strategy I:	+5%	−5%
Strategy II:	+5%	−5%
Strategy III:	+100%	−100%

Figure 5.1   Leveraged investing.

Consider a pension fund that invested in the Japanese stock market at its peak of about 40,000 yen in 1989. The market fell over the next two years to a low of about 16,000 yen, or a 60 percent decline.

If the pension fund bought shares of Japanese stocks in a conventional way, it lost 60 percent of its investment. If the pension fund used derivatives by buying an index future in Japanese stocks of exactly the same face value, keeping in the margin account or other reserve for this investment the same amount of cash, it also lost 60 percent of its investment. However, if the pension fund bought the index future in the same amount, with a margin deposit or other reserve for this investment of only 5 percent of the total value of the stocks covered by the index (using 20-to-1 leverage), its percentage losses on the margin amount invested would be much higher—in fact, 20 times higher. Consider the purchase of 40,000 yen worth of stocks represented by the index.

If the investment was made on an unleveraged basis, the pension fund would have deposited in its margin account and the reserves it kept for the trade a total of 40,000 yen. As the index dropped to 16,000 yen, the loss would have been 40,000 yen less 16,000 yen, or 24,000 yen, which is 60 percent of the initial cash margin and reserves of 40,000 yen.

If 20-to-1 leverage was used, the pension fund would have kept in its margin account and reserves only 2,000 yen for each 40,000 yen represented by the index. As the index dropped to 16,000 yen, the loss would still have been 40,000 yen less 16,000 yen, or 24,000 yen. This loss amounts to 1,200 percent of the cash margin and reserves of 2,000 yen set aside for the trade. The use of 20-to-1 leverage multiplied the percentage losses by 20 as well; the 1,200 percent loss at 20-to-1 leverage is 20 times the 60 percent loss without leverage.

We have assumed that the pension fund dedicated only 2,000 yen to its investment in Japanese stocks, using 20-to-1 leverage. Doing so, it lost 1,200 percent of the original 2,000 yen, or a total of 24,000 yen. The additional 22,000 yen it lost, over and above its original 2,000 yen dedicated to the trade, had to come from somewhere. The pension fund would have had to liquidate other investments, not originally dedicated to this trade, in order to come up with the 22,000 yen required to meet the margin calls from the futures exchange as its investments were marked to market on a daily basis. If the pension fund finally ran out of money to meet these margin calls, it would be bankrupt. Hopefully, it would have cut its losses by ending its highly leveraged investment in the Japanese stock market long before that happened.

In fact, the old London merchant banking firm of Baring Brothers found itself unexpectedly in exactly this situation, and wired over $800,000,000 to the Singapore futures exchange in about one month to cover margin calls on very highly leveraged Japanese stock index investments in early 1995. Baring's ran out of money; the firm's debts exceeded its assets, and it was quickly sold to a Dutch company willing to assume those debts. The owners of Baring's lost their company as a result.

HEDGING, SPECULATING, AND MIXED APPLICATIONS

Whether high or low leverage is used, whether the activity is called investing or speculating, any investment in Japanese stocks, or for that matter in stocks in the United States, involves the possibility of gain or loss. Because of this risk, investing in stocks is sometimes referred to as *speculative,* and the use of derivatives to invest in stocks is speculative as well. This is so whether the leverage is 1 to 1, so that the risks are no more speculative than buying stocks directly, or if the leverage is 20 to 1, with risks and opportunity for reward 20 times as high as a direct investment in stocks.

Hedging with derivatives involves exactly the opposite: avoiding risks rather than taking risks. The hedger is by definition reducing risk. To the extent the hedger is not reducing risk, he or she is speculating, not hedging. Sometimes, in practice, the business and investment situation can be so complex that it is difficult to tell how much of a given position involves a hedge and how much involves speculation, but the conceptual distinction is clear.

Suppose Thales' contract was a futures contract, and not an option. The owners of the olive presses were hedgers—they were renting their presses at a fixed rate in the future, guaranteeing themselves a fixed profit whether the season was outstanding or terrible. They chose to fix their profit now rather than to take the risk of a bad season when their presses might not be used or to count on a good season when they could rent their presses at much higher rates. They were limiting both their risk and their opportunity for reward.

Thales, as we know, was a speculator, since he owned no olive trees whose crop of olives would have to be pressed. If he had been an olive grower entering the same contracts, the contracts would have been a hedge against the possibility of having to pay a high price for olive presses come harvesttime. Grain farmers who sell their corn on the futures market today make a very similar decision. They sell the crop in the futures market, fixing their sales price in advance, so that their only concern is with farming, producing the crop for sale, and not with predicting whether prices will be high or low on the day they come to market.

The distinction between speculating and hedging can become subtle when more complicated derivatives are examined and when derivatives are considered in light of the emphasis on diversification under modern portfolio theory. Just as grain producers can hedge against the risk of a price drop, so portfolio managers can hedge against various risks of their portfolios. Portfolio managers can hedge against the risk of a particular stock, for example by buying a put on that stock, or they can attempt to hedge against broader risks of the portfolio, which are less clearly defined. In fact, the modern laws applicable to fiduciaries, based on modern portfolio theory of finance, require fiduciaries to consider the risk and return of the portfolio as a whole, in addition to that of each particular investment alone. When derivatives are included in a portfolio, they become part of this calculation like any other investment, even when they are not being used as a hedge against the risks associated with any particular asset. The extent to which a derivative is a hedge depends on its relationship with the rest of the portfolio.

If a portfolio contains no stock except 1,000 shares of General Motors, and the portfolio manager purchases a put on 1,000 shares of General Motors, this is clearly a hedge. It reduces the risk of price declines in the General Motors stock, at the cost of the premium paid to purchase the put option. If the portfolio manager purchases a put on 2,000 shares of General Motors stock, however, only 1,000 shares of the purchase constitutes a hedge, and the additional 1,000 shares is a speculative investment. This will produce a profit if the price of General Motors falls sufficiently to cover the premium. If not, the investor will lose part or all of the time premium paid for the options.

If the portfolio contains 1,000 shares of the stock of Ford Motor Company, as well as 1,000 shares of General Motors stock, the purchase of a put on 1,000 shares of GM is still a hedge, since it hedges the portfolio's specific risk in GM stock. However, the purchase of a put on 2,000 shares of GM stock now requires a more complex analysis. The first half of the put is a hedge against the GM stock (1,000 shares of GM versus a put on 1,000 shares of GM). The put on the other 1,000 shares of GM stock is no longer a simple speculation, however, because there are 1,000 shares of Ford stock in the portfolio. The put on GM shares offers some hedging protection for the Ford shares, since the price of Ford and GM tend to fluctuate up and down together. If car sales are down, and the price of automobile manufacturers' stock declines, the drop in the price of Ford shares will be offset to some extent by the profit on the extra puts on GM stock. To that extent, the extra GM puts are a hedge against the Ford stock. However, GM and Ford stock prices are unlikely to fall by exactly the same percentage, so GM puts are an imperfect hedge against Ford stock. To some extent, they constitute a hedge against the Ford stock, and to some extent they constitute a speculation that GM stock will decline more than the Ford stock, so that the profits on the GM puts will be even greater than the losses on the Ford stock.

No one can be sure in advance just how much of the investment in the extra GM puts is a hedge against the Ford stock, and how much is a speculation that GM will decline more than Ford in a bad market for automotive stocks, because no one knows in advance what the relative decline of Ford and GM will be in a bear market. Of course, past behavior of the two stocks can be studied, along with current market conditions, but the resulting prediction is no more certain than a weather forecast. Consequently, the extent to which the purchase of the extra 1,000 puts is a hedge, and the extent to which it is a speculation, cannot be determined with precision.

The point of this example applies to most portfolios containing a variety of stocks, which do not exactly mirror the contents of indexes such as the S&P 500. Therefore, purchase of index put options on the Standard & Poor's 500 index, which can be used to hedge the risk of stock portfolios, is almost never a perfect hedge against the risks inherent in the portfolio. Even if the face amount of the puts exactly matches the market value of the stocks in the portfolio, there still remains the speculative element of whether the decline in the value of those stocks will be greater or less than the decline in the S&P 500 index.

To create a somewhat more perfect hedge, an investor could purchase a number of put options matched to specific investments, and attempt to hedge some or all of the residual risk of the entire portfolio through a more broadly based derivative. For example, a manager with a portfolio containing Ford and GM stock and 300 other stocks might hedge the GM stock with GM puts, buy extra GM puts as a partial hedge against the Ford stock and a partial speculation that GM will decline faster than Ford, and take a short futures position on the Standard & Poor's 500 stocks as a partial hedge against the 300 other stocks in the portfolio and a partial speculation that those particular stocks are so well selected that they will rise faster and lose value slower than the Standard & Poor's 500 stocks. Determining in advance just how much of the derivative position is speculation and how much is a hedge can only be an approximation.

Hedges can also be directly designed into corporate financing decisions as a partial hedge against business risks. For example, a company that depends heavily on petroleum products as a raw material may purchase crude oil futures as a hedge. If oil prices go up, the extra cost it will face in buying petroleum products will be offset by its profits on crude oil futures. Alternatively, the company could also issue new debt in which the interest payments the company makes to its lenders vary inversely with an index based on the price of crude oil. If oil prices rise so that the company must pay more for its raw materials, these increased costs will be offset by decreased interest costs on the company's debt. The debt security itself now acts as a hedge against oil price changes. As in the previous example, the hedge is not exact, but contains elements of speculation as well, since the prices of the raw materials purchased by the company probably will not vary exactly with the prices of crude oil.

FINANCIAL ENGINEERING

A few examples of financially engineered products have already been presented in some detail in the discussion of the development of currency swaps, multicurrency-linked securities, and the use of collateralized mortgage obligations (CMOs and REMICs) to make mortgage-backed securities marketable to investors who wish to take greater or lesser shares of the repayment risk and other characteristics of the underlying mortgages. Financial engineering is the aspect of derivatives that has spawned the greatest creativity of application and most excited people's imaginations. As one commentator has suggested, it presents the opportunity of a "derivative reality," a virtual world of business and finance where, although risk and reward cannot be eliminated, it can be reconfigured and tailored to any need, and the boundaries between corporations and states can be erased in economic terms by the financial wizardry of the "rocket scientists" who have become investment bankers.

The growth of complex derivatives owes much to modern finance theory and to the speed, power, and widespread availability of computers. More complex pricing models and mathematical risk modeling may allow traditional business and finance operations to operate in more efficient ways and to more accurately evaluate the risks of various opportunities. And if the risk can be measured more accurately, it may be possible to take risks in a more selective and appropriate manner. In the aggregate, this may lead to a more optimal risk/return profile—but derivatives cannot, ultimately, separate risk from return.

Derivatives may also open new arbitrage opportunities by decreasing transaction costs and facilitating the use of high, inexpensive leverage. For example, as discussed in chapter 2, currency swaps have allowed corporations to obtain financing in foreign countries at lower rates than they could otherwise. Predictably, as that or any other arbitrage strategy becomes more common, the benefits are reduced.

Such opportunities require careful analysis and handling to ensure they do not involve unexpected risks; but businesses do not become successful without taking some risks. Being in business involves taking a calculated risk when the right opportunity presents itself. If derivatives allow the risk to be more carefully tailored to the needs of the business, or permit the business to exploit an otherwise unexploitable opportunity, they are an invaluable tool. Of course, there is the risk of using them improperly. We will discuss ways to avoid this risk in chapter 12.

6

Hedging a Stock Portfolio

Futures and options are often used to hedge stock portfolios. This is a good example for a detailed look at hedging because it is easy to understand, and the same methods apply to any sort of hedging. They can be used by a bank or company treasurer dealing with financial instruments such as foreign and domestic bonds, or by a businessperson trying to control costs for industrial commodities such as copper and oil, or by a producer or consumer of agricultural commodities such as wheat and sugar. In all cases, the same principles apply.

Options are available on many, but not all, specific stocks, and are also available on various stock indexes and index futures. Futures contracts are publicly traded on the S&P 500 index and a few other indexes, but not on individual stocks. However, the equivalent of a futures contract can be constructed on any asset where options are traded, through the creation of a "synthetic future" long position by buying a call and selling a put, or a "synthetic future" short position by buying a put and selling a call, a technique that will be discussed in this chapter.

A portfolio of stocks can be fully or partially hedged. If an investor wants to keep the stocks but eliminate the risks, he or she will fully hedge the portfolio. Using put options, the investor may limit the risk of a major loss while keeping all of the upside potential less the premium paid for the puts. If futures are used instead of options, the economic effect may be close to that of a sale of the portfolio. However, the investor may prefer a hedge to a sale. For example, the investor may have grown uncomfortable with the risk of the stocks in current market conditions, but realize that if the paper profits were taken by selling the stocks, substantial taxes would be due. Of course, any hedge that limits the downside risk involves a price, which might be paid as a cash option premium equivalent to an insurance premium, or by foregoing some amount of upside potential.

In considering whether to hedge, an investor may be concerned about the portfolio's exposure to two types of risk: (1) the *specific risk* that a particular stock will drop in price and (2) the *systemic risk* that all stocks will drop in value.

In hedging the stock portfolio, the investor has available three tools, which we have discussed in general terms: futures, options, and swaps. In this chapter, we will consider specific ways in which these tools can be applied to hedge the stock portfolio. The problem is the same whether the stock portfolio is $1 million or $10 billion in size. The details of implementation may vary, however. For example, it is more difficult to hedge a portfolio of tens of billions of dollars, simply because purchases of futures or options in the size necessary could overwhelm the market on any given trading day. Exchanges also have position limits which limit the size of the transaction that can be done.

As we will discuss in later chapters, the same principles can also be applied to hedging business risks. As business risks are likely to be more varied and specific to the particular business transaction, the tools and methods of implementing these solutions may be more specialized. The principles, however, remain very similar.

HEDGING WITH FUTURES

Futures contracts are traded on a variety of stock indexes. These indexes may be broad indexes such as the S&P 500 (based on the values of 500 selected stocks), or they may be more specialized indexes such as the biotech index (based on biotechnology companies) or the Russell 2000 (based on 2,000 small stocks). A futures hedge is therefore not likely to perfectly hedge the risk of a particular stock or group of stocks in a particular portfolio. However, futures contracts provide a good way to neutralize potential losses or gains from broad stock market movements, while retaining the possibility of gains (or losses) as a result of the particular stocks in the investor's portfolio outperforming (or underperforming) the general market. In this way, the investor can keep the specific opportunities associated with particular stocks, while hedging out the systemic risk of the market as a whole.

As an example, suppose the investor decides to use S&P 500 futures as a hedge against the various stock in his or her portfolio, currently worth $1 million. The futures contract on the S&P 500 index is written so that it changes in value by $500 for each 1-point move in the S&P 500 index. If that index is now approximately 500, each contract represents the value of about $250,000 worth of the S&P 500 stocks ($500 per point times the 500-point value of the index equals $250,000). Four contracts would represent four times that value, or $1 million. By selling four S&P 500 futures contracts, the investor has, in effect, sold short $1 million worth of the stocks in the Standard & Poor's 500 index. Assuming that S&P 500 futures can be purchased at margin requirements of around 10-to-1 leverage, shorting four contracts would thus require a margin of around 10 percent of the $1 million face value, or a margin deposit of $100,000.

Since the investor has sold (or gone short on) the futures contracts, the investor will profit from them if the value of the index of the stock declines. If the S&P 500 falls by 10 percent, the investor will make a profit of 10 percent of $1 million, or $100,000. Because the investor is leveraged 10 to 1, the value of his or her futures account with the broker will rise by $100,000, to a total of $200,000.

At the same time, if the stock market in general has fallen, the value of the stocks in the investor's portfolio is likely to have fallen as well—but not necessarily to the same extent. Stocks tend to rise and fall together, but there is still substantial variation. With this hedge against systemic risk in place, the investor will prosper or lose depending not upon whether the market itself rises or falls, but upon whether the stocks in the investor's portfolio rise or fall more or less than the rest of the market. In figure 6.1, the first chart shows the returns of an individual stock (ABC), and the returns of the S&P 500 Index futures. If ABC is hedged by shorting an equivalent amount of futures, the return will be the difference between the two, illustrated by the second chart. The investor will profit or lose to the extent the individual stock outperforms or underperforms the index.

If the market rises by 10 percent, the price of the S&P 500 futures will rise by 50 points. At $500 a point times 50 points, this will be a loss of $25,000 on each contract. Since there are four contracts, the total loss will be $100,000 on the four S&P 500 contracts that were sold short. To cover the loss, the investor will have to deposit an additional $100,000 into the futures account.

Portfolio: 100,000 Shares of ABC
Hedge: Short equivalent amount S&P 500 Index Futures Contracts

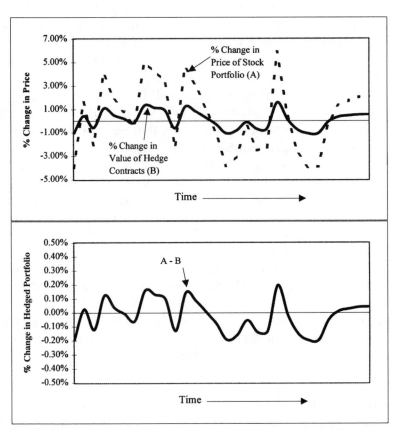

Figure 6.1   Hedging with index futures.

If while the market was going up 10 percent, the stocks in the investor's portfolio went up 15 percent, the value of the stock account will have increased from $1 million to $1.15 million. Between the stocks in the stock account and the S&P 500 position in the futures account, there is a net profit of $50,000 (equal to $150,000 profit in the stock account less $100,000 loss in the futures account). This profit of $50,000, or 5 percent, is exactly the extent by which the investor's stocks outperformed the stock market as a whole, rising 15 percent while the market rose only 10 percent.

The same 5 percent profit would result if the market fell by 10 percent while the investor's stocks fell by only 5 percent. Five percent loss in the investor's stocks would be $50,000 (5 percent of the original $1 million value), while a 10 percent fall in the stock market would yield a $100,000 profit in the short position on the S&P 500 (10 percent of the original 500-point index value is 50 points. Multiplying the 50 points by $500 a point is $25,000 profit per contract times four contracts is $100,000).

Conversely, if the investor's stocks underperform the stock market by 5 percent, there will be a $50,000 loss, whether the market is rising or falling. If the investor's stocks rise only 5 percent while the market rises 10 percent, there will be a $100,000 loss on the four futures contracts, and a profit of only $50,000 on the stocks, for a net loss of $50,000. Likewise, if the investor's stocks fall 10 percent while the stock market as a whole falls only 5 percent, there will be a $100,000 loss in the stock account, offset only in part by a $50,000 profit on the four futures contracts in the futures account.

It may appear that this sort of strategy requires a substantial pool of capital to buy the futures and keep up with margin calls, but many brokers can limit this capital requirement by creating a sort of virtual link between the stock and the futures account. If the broker handling the stock account has an affiliated futures commission merchant who deals in futures, it may be particularly convenient for the investor to open a futures account by taking out a margin loan against the stock. Because of the stock collateral, the investor will get fairly reasonable rates on the loan. For example, the investor might pay at the rate of 7 percent a year for the margin loan, or $7,000 on the $100,000 loan. The $7,000 cost of maintaining the account is only 0.7 percent of the $1 million stock portfolio being hedged. This is the net financing cost of maintaining the hedging account for the $1 million portfolio, before considering the gains, losses, and transaction expenses of the hedge.

HEDGING WITH PUTS

By using put options rather than futures, the hedger can keep the opportunity to profit if the stock rises in price, at the cost of the premium paid to buy the put option as insurance. In this way, the investor will profit if the investor's portfolio goes up, not just if they outperform the general market. As an example, consider a portfolio containing 14,000 shares of Philip Morris stock selling at 73.875. At that price, the stock is worth $1,034,250. Suppose the portfolio manager fears a loss in the stock, either because of a general stock market crash or because of factors peculiar to that stock, such as pending litigation or recent regulatory proposals. Either way, the manager wants to hedge the risk.

Looking in the newspaper in August, the portfolio manager discovers that the December put option with a strike price of 70 is selling at 2¼. (The option price quoted in the newspaper is not necessarily the price that you will pay in a purchase the next morning. Usually, both a bid and ask price are quoted, and the price at which you will buy the option is somewhere in between. Also, you will have to pay a commission on the option purchase. For purposes of this example, these costs are included in the option cost used. They must, of course, be taken into account in any calculation.) This would give the manager the right to sell the stock for 70 in December even if it had fallen far below that price. Each put option covers 100 shares, so the price of each option would therefore be 100 times the 2.25 price quoted in the newspaper, or $225. (Each option covers 100 shares, but the price of the option contract is quoted on the basis of a single share.) Since each option covers 100 shares, the portfolio manager would need 140 options to cover the 14,000 shares. The total for 140 put option contracts at $225 each would be $140 \times 225 = \$31,500$.

So, for an option premium of $31,500 the stock can be hedged until December at a strike price of 70. The out-of-pocket cost of $31,500 is 3.046 percent of the present market value of the Philip Morris stock, which is $1,034,250.

Since the option covers only one-third of a year, the annualized out-of-pocket cost of the hedge is about 9.14 percent, or three times the cost of hedging for one-third of the year, assuming that as each option expires, a new put option can be bought at a similar cost. This annualized cost is a rough approximation at best, since the market price of Philip Morris stock is likely to be either higher or lower when the new option is purchased, so the risk being hedged at that time will be a different risk, and the cost of the hedge will also be somewhat different.

Philip Morris is one of a small number of stocks on which long-term options, called LEAPS, are available. (LEAPS is an acronym for long-term equity anticipation securities.) If the portfolio manager doesn't want to have to worry about buying new options every four months when the old ones expire, he or she could purchase a LEAPS put option on Philip Morris at the same strike price of 70, but expiring a year from January, or 17 months in the future. The price of this option, on the same day as the aforementioned prices, is quoted in the newspaper at 5.75. The cost of 140 options covering 100 shares each, or 14,000 shares in total, would therefore be 14,000 times 5.75, or $80,500. This amounts to 7.8 percent of the total market value of the shares, but this option covers one year and five months, rather than only four months in total, so that the annualized cost of the LEAPS option is only 5.5 percent, compared to 9.3 percent for the sequence of shorter-duration options.

This big difference in the cost of the option, depending on the time period, is not unusual. Sometimes longer-term options are relatively more expensive, sometimes less. In any case, the closer the option gets to expiration, the faster the time premium tends to erode.

Costs of Hedging:
The Time Premium and the Deductible

If the LEAPS put option is held to its expiration date a year from January, the investor will lose all of the option insurance premium of $80,500, or 5.5 percent of the value of the stock. This loss will reduce any profits from dividends that have been received during the period and any gains that might have been made on price increases in the Philip Morris stock. It is like homeowners insurance, a cost that must be paid for protection whether or not the house burns down. As it is an option that has been purchased (rather than sold), the premium is also the maximum that can be lost.

Like insurance, this option also has a deductible—a certain amount of loss that must be borne by the investor before the "insurance" takes effect. The strike price of the option is 70, so that if the price of Philip Morris stock is 70 a year from January, there will be a loss on the stock that is not covered by the option insurance. The stock is trading at 73.875 today, so that loss will be 73.875 less 70, or 3.875 per share. Since there are 14,000 shares, the total "deductible" will be 14,000 times 3.875, or $54,250. This amounts to 5.2 percent of the market value of the stock today. (See figure 6.2.)

If the stock is trading at 70 a year from January, the time premium of $80,500 will have been paid, and there will also be a loss of $54,250 on the stock because of the deductible. The total value of the stockholding after taking into account the cost of the put option insurance will be $134,750 less than it is today: a 13 percent loss on the stock position, estimated at roughly 9.2 percent per year on an annualized basis.

Of course, $54,250 of this loss would have been suffered even if the option had not been purchased; it is simply due to the decline in value of the stock. And if the stock is trading below 70 a year from

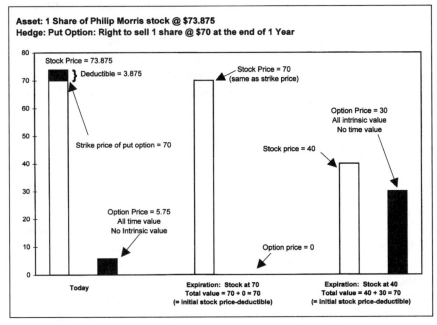

Figure 6.2   Hedging—time premium and deductible.

January, the value of the option will begin to be felt. If, for example, the stock is selling at $40 per share, the profit from the option will be $339,500, even net of the $80,500 time premium that was paid. The total value of the stockholding (the stock, the value of the option, and its cost) will be $134,750 less than it is today—the same as if the stock had fallen to 70, 60, or lower. Without the hedge, the loss would have been $474,250 (today's price of 73.875 less the drop to a price of 40 is a loss of 33.875 per share times 14,000 shares). The hedge saves $339,500, or over 70 percent of the loss, even after paying the time premium of $80,500 and the deductible of $54,250.

This type of fall is not impossible. Even though Philip Morris is one of the largest and most highly regarded American companies, and even though it pays a good dividend, regulatory and litigation risks and price competition have made its stock volatile. At different times in the 1990s, the value of Philip Morris stock has fallen by half, and has also doubled. A portfolio manager might well decide that a 5.5 percent annual time premium is a reasonable price to pay for insurance against the possibility of a major loss. Furthermore, by continuing to hold the stock with a put option in place, the investor continues to receive the dividends from Philip Morris, which in some cases may pay most of the time premium. With the hedge in place, the portfolio manager can be assured that there will be no catastrophic loss in the value of the stock. On the other hand, if the stock increases greatly in value, which it also has done in the past, this increase can be captured for the portfolio.

Exercising the Option

As a practical matter, this strategy does not require the manager to exercise options. That is, the investor does not need to actually sell the stock at the strike price of 70 to gain its benefit. The option itself can be sold before expiration, capturing any increase in its value. This is important, because selling the stock could have adverse tax consequences if the stock were to increase greatly in value since its original purchase, perhaps many years before the hedge was entered. Selling the stock would result in tax recognition of the gain and the payment of substantial capital gains taxes. Indeed, this tax consequence may itself be a reason for hedging the stock rather than selling it.

Of course, even if the put options themselves are sold rather than exercised to sell the stocks, there are tax consequences. A gain in the value of the option, offsetting paper losses on sale of the stock, results in taxable gain on which taxes must be paid. If there is a tax loss on the stock, some of the stock might be sold to offset this gain, but this strategy will not be available if the stock was originally purchased at a price far below its present market value. Another way to mitigate this is to purchase options with a very distant expiration date, such as LEAPS or privately negotiated options. The option might then be sold, and the gain recognized, in a year in which there are other tax losses to offset the gains. The option position can then be reestablished, again with a distant expiration date, to protect the stocks.

If the investor purchases an option, the investor can decide whether and when to exercise it. If the investor sells an option, however, the party to whom it has been sold makes this decision, so that the timing of the exercise can be unpredictable for the selling investor. Most stock options, index options, and options on futures can in theory be exercised. (American-style options can be exercised at any time; European-style options can only be exercised at the time of their expiration. Both these styles can be traded on American or European exchanges.) In practice, however, very few options are ever exercised. As expiration date approaches, owners of options tend to sell them; those who have sold options tend to buy them back; and the result is a liquidation of the options by cash payments rather than exercise. Moreover, some options can never be exercised at all and must be settled at their expiration by a cash payment reflecting their value. This is typical of the "index options" traded on the stock exchanges, on indexes such as the S&P 100.

Eliminating the Deductible:
In-the-Money Options

Some costs of hedging with options may be reduced by hedging with in-the-money options. This not only eliminates the deductible, but may reduce the time premium as well. However, these options require a larger cash outlay because they include intrinsic value, and this intrinsic value can be lost.

For example, instead of hedging the Philip Morris stock position with puts with a strike price of 70 and expiring in four months, the hedge could have involved puts with a strike price of 75, also expiring in four months. The 70 puts cost 2.25, while the 75 puts cost 5.625. However, the 75 puts include some intrinsic value. In our example, the Philip Morris stock was selling at 73.875 in the open market. The 75 puts give the buyer the right to sell Philip Morris stock at 75, which is 1.125 above its current market price. The owner of the put option can buy the stock at 73.875 in the open market and sell it through the put option for 75, so the intrinsic value of the put option is therefore 1.125. Of course, since the price of the put option is higher than its intrinsic value, the owner of the option would never exercise it in this way; more value can be realized simply by selling the put option itself in the open market. (See figure 6.3.)

The market price of the option is made up of two components: (1) intrinsic value of 1.125 and (2) the balance of the option price, which consists of the time premium, just like the time premium for the out-of-the-money options discussed previously. The further the strike price is from the current market price, the smaller the time premium, whether the option is in the money or out of the money. This tends to make out-of-the-money options very

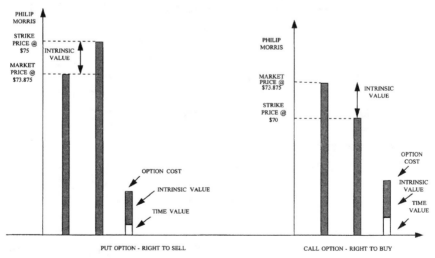

Figure 6.3 Calls and puts at purchase.

cheap, if their strike price is distant from the current market price. In the case of an in-the-money option, however, distance from the strike price increases the intrinsic value dollar for dollar, so that options with distant strike prices are very expensive, even if their time premium is very small. The intrinsic value accounts for almost all of the market price.

If hedging is conducted with in-the-money options, there is no deductible. Any decrease in the value of the stock will cause an increase in the intrinsic value of the option. However, if the value of the stock increases past the exercise price, in this case 75, the option is out of the money and all the intrinsic value is lost. There is no deductible, but the loss of intrinsic value will reduce gains if the hedged asset increases in value.

OPTION PRICING: THEORETICAL MODELS

The time premium of an option can vary widely, depending on the supply and demand for the option, which in turn is affected by traders' expectations concerning the *volatility* of the price of the asset underlying the option; that is, how likely it is that the price of the underlying asset will fluctuate greatly. The greater the volatility of a stock, the more likely it is to reach the strike price of an option. For example, if Philip Morris schedules a press conference for a "very important announcement," traders may well expect that the announcement will have a big effect on the price of the stock, causing it to either rise or fall, and so the time premium for options will greatly increase, just as the expected volatility of the Philip Morris stock has increased due to the announced press conference. A stock with a high historic volatility will, in general, have options with a higher time premium. Historical changes in volatility of the underlying asset are therefore tracked carefully by traders. If a contract trades between 45 and 55 over a period of time, with a mean of 50, its historical volatility over that period would be 10 percent, since the price varied from 10 percent below 50 to 10 percent above 50.

The *implied volatility* of options is calculated by applying a theoretical model to current market prices of the underlying asset and options with different strike prices and expiration dates. The mathematical model determines the "fair value" of each option compared to other options on the same underlying asset and the current price of that asset. These values also imply a volatility level for the underlying asset or index on which the options are written; this implied volatility level can be compared with past implied volatility levels and with the historical volatility of the underlying asset to see whether option prices are suggesting that the contract or index is expected to be more volatile or less volatile than it has been in the past.

Development of the Black-Scholes mathematical model spurred much interest in computerized analysis of options pricing, and work continues to be done on such models and the mathematical assumptions underlying them. For example, the original Black-Scholes formula involved an assumption that stock price probabilities fit a lognormal pattern; that they fit the familiar bell curve, permitting mathematically elegant valuation formulas. Recent work, however, suggests that this assumption may be invalid, and that the probability of big gains or losses is greater than a lognormal distribution would suggest. A serious student of option pricing faces many intricate mathematical challenges, and there is no universal agreement on the correct formulas for the analysis. Nevertheless, the Black-Scholes formula has been adopted by the FASB (Federal Accounting Standard Board) for its marking-to-market model.

Investors can easily determine the market price of an option. The newspaper quotes the last price at which the option traded at the end of the day. Throughout the trading day, brokers will provide *bid* prices, at which an option can be sold, and *asked* prices, at which it can be purchased. The size of the spread between bid and asked varies during the day, depending on the level of activity in that particular option contract; more buyers and sellers drive the spread to narrower levels.

HEDGING A STOCK WITH SYNTHETIC FUTURES: BUYING A PUT, SELLING A CALL

Buying a put protects the investor from losses while preserving the benefits of any gains on the stock. If the portfolio manager doesn't believe that Philip Morris stock is likely to rise in the near future, he or she may not wish to pay the cost of the option insurance, since there will likely be no gains to offset the cost. One obvious solution in such a case is simply to sell the stock. But there may be reasons why the portfolio manager would not want to sell the stock. For example, if the stock is in a portfolio that pays taxes rather than in a tax-free pension trust, and if there has been a large gain on the stock, the manager may not want to sell the stock and pay the taxes now. Another reason to keep the stock may be high dividends. Or, in some cases, there may be restrictions on selling the stock as a matter of securities law or of contract. For example, when one corporation acquires another, some of the purchase price may be paid to the shareholders of the second corporation in the form of stock in the first corporation. In some cases, there may be restrictions on the manner and rate at which such stock may be sold in order to prevent the market price from being depressed by the sudden appearance of large quantities of stock for sale.

One alternative to selling the stock is to short a future contract on the stock, but futures for specific stocks are not traded in the public markets. An index future could be sold short, but this only hedges out the risk of general market movements, not the risks associated with a specific stock.

In these circumstances, the manager may wish to create a *synthetic future* by buying a put on the stock and offsetting its cost by selling a call at the same strike price. The put will protect against a loss in the stock, and selling the call will offset the cost of the put's time premium but eliminate the possibility of gains on the stock. This strategy allows the portfolio manager to continue to collect the dividends on the stock and defer adverse consequences of selling the stock, such as taxation of gains. In other words, it acts like a synthetic future. If the portfolio manager later decides the stock is likely to rise substantially in value, he or she can remove the hedge altogether or convert it to a simple put option hedge by closing the call transaction.

Let us examine how this works. Returning to our Philip Morris example, the portfolio manager would, in addition to buying the January LEAPS put with a strike price of 70 for 5¾s, sell a January LEAPS call at the same strike price of 70. In effect, the manager is buying insurance against a decline in value and offsetting its cost by selling the opportunity for profit through the sale of the call option. The person buying this call will have the right to buy the stock at 70 even if the market value of the stock has increased greatly above that price.

The LEAPS call with a 70 strike price expiring a year from January is currently selling at a price of 9. If the current market price is 73.875, this call option is already in the money by 3.875, so that the price of 9 is made up of intrinsic value of 3.875 and a time premium of 5.125. By selling a call, the portfolio manager will receive $9 per share, which will more than offset the $5.75 per share paid out for the put option. In fact, the manager will collect $3.25 per share on the transaction—$45,500 on a 14,000-share transaction. The manager will, however, have to maintain a margin deposit against the call which was sold. As you may remember, selling, rather than buying, a call or a put involves much greater exposure to loss than the actual cost of the call or put. As the price of the stock increases, so does the loss on the call. However, since the portfolio manager already owns 14,000 shares of Philip Morris stock, he or she is writing a *covered call*. If the stock surges to new highs, losses on the call will offset gains on the stock, but the manager will not suffer any uncovered losses.

If the price of Philip Morris stock is lower when the option expires than it is today, the loss on the stock will be offset by the profit on the put option. If the Philip Morris stock is higher on option expiration than it is today, the gain on the stock will be offset by a loss on the call sold by the portfolio manager. The result of the transaction is very similar to that of selling the stock, except that the manager continues to collect the dividend on the stock. Also, the manager will not face the tax consequences of selling the stock.

There is a small cost to the option position the portfolio manager has taken, however. If the price of the stock is 70 when the options expire, for example, the loss will be 3.875 per share on the stock itself, or $54,250 (73.875 less 70 times 14,000 shares). Since the strike price of the put is 70, there will be no profit on the put to offset this loss. However, there will be no loss on the call at that point, since the strike price of the call is also 70. The portfolio manager will be able to keep the entire profit of $45,500 collected when the option position was entered, and this will partly offset the $54,250 loss of the deductible. The maximum loss on the position will be $54,250 less $45,500, or $8,750, which itself is much less than the loss of $54,250 that would have been incurred had the hedge position not been entered. So the cost of the option position is less than 1 percent of the $1,034,250 market value of the shares. This cost is only a fraction of the dividends that will be received during the time period.

Like hedging with futures, hedging with synthetic futures is inexpensive, but it also leaves very little profit potential. It is useful when there is some special tax situation that may be improved if the shares are sold in the future rather than today, or if it is regarded as a low-cost way to avoid exposure to the stock during a period of uncertainty, with the idea of modifying the hedge at a later time when the potential rewards of the stock appear to be greater.

This particular option position is sometimes called a synthetic future because it produces economic results that are the same as those of a futures position. It is a way of creating a future position in any security or index where there is no futures contract offered on the exchange, but options are traded. In this particular example, the position created was equivalent to a short future position in that the option position gains value if the price of the stock declines, and loses value if the price of the stock increases.

A synthetic *long* future can be constructed by buying a call and selling a put—the exact opposite of the synthetic *short* position. The purchase of a call gives an opportunity to profit from price increases, while the sale of the put takes in a time premium which offsets the time premium paid out for the call. The sale of the put, of course, also exposes the investor to loss should the value of the investment fall (the buyer of the put will have the right to sell the stock at the exercise price of the put even if the current market value falls below that price). This combination of puts and calls is, in effect, equivalent to a long future position, since the investor profits from price increases, loses from price declines, and pays little or no net time premium. It can be used as an alternative to investing in the stock (with the possibility of greater leverage), or as a hedge against a short stock position.

A close equivalent to hedging a stock with synthetic futures through the use of options is the time-honored tactic of *shorting against the box,* which is even closer to selling the stock while deferring the tax consequences of a sale. An owner of 14,000 shares of Philip Morris stock in a brokerage account could simply sell short 14,000 shares of Philip Morris stock in the same brokerage account. Unlike the synthetic futures hedge, the investor would no longer be receiving any net dividends on the Philip Morris stock, since the dividends received on the stock owned in the account would have to be paid out again on the stock sold short in the account. Instead, however, the investor could negotiate with the broker to receive interest on the cash received from the short sale of the stock.

Synthetic futures provide more flexibility than shorting against the box. Using options, an investor can select strike prices of the put purchased or the call sold, at varying distances from the current market price, so as to retain more of the economic risk or reward of the rise or fall of the stock price. This is called a *collar,* since the strike price of the put limits the amount of loss, and the strike price of the call limits the amount of gain—all net of the option premium received for selling the call, less the option premium paid when buying the put. In figure 6.4 the upper charts illustrate the effect of a put option hedge, while the lower charts illustrate the effect of a hedge collar.

HEDGING INDUSTRY RISK WITH SYNTHETIC FUTURES

In an earlier example, we saw how futures can be used to hedge against systemic risk, eliminating both the risk and potential

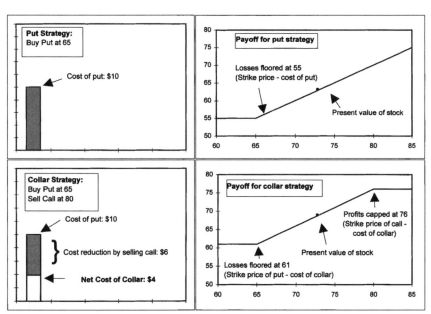

The cost of hedging a portfolio with a put option can be reduced by selling a call. However, this also means giving up some opportunity for gain. By setting the strike price for the put and the call a distance from the strike price, some opportunity for profit can be retained. Payoff values are shown at expiration, and therefore do not include any time value.

Figure 6.4   Collar hedge.

profit associated with general movements of the stock market up and down, and leaving the investor with the opportunity to profit or lose only insofar as his or her own specific investments outperform the stock market as a whole. We also saw how options can hedge against systemic risk, leaving profit potential open, at the cost of an option premium. Next, we saw how options or synthetic futures can be used to more perfectly hedge the risk of a single stock. In fact, options can also be used to create synthetic futures which can be used to redefine the investment even more specifically. For example, the investment can be structured so that a stock is protected from a general decline in its sector of the market by put options on that sector, or so that an investor will gain or lose to the extent that a particular stock, or portfolio of stocks, outperforms a particular sector of the market.

An investor who owns a stock, or a portfolio of stocks, believing they will outperform a particular industry sector, can hedge against the risk of a price decline in that industry. This can be accomplished quite easily if options are traded on an index of stocks in that industry. By buying put options on that index, the investor can hedge against a general decline in that market sector, leaving open the profit opportunity, less the premium paid for the put options. Of course, the investor is not protected from a fall in value in his or her particular stocks, unless that fall is accompanied by a general decline in the market sector. Alternatively, without bearing the cost of an option premium, the investor can buy a put and sell a call on the index, creating a synthetic short position in the industry, so that the investor will profit or lose only to the extent that the particular stock or portfolio outperforms or underperforms the industry.

Even if no index options are traded, the investor can reach a similar result by buying puts and selling calls on a large number of stocks in the industry, creating a synthetic short position in the industry against the investor's existing long position in a particular stock or group of stocks in the industry. Of course, this is more complex than using industry options or futures that already exist, and the availability of the technique is limited to stocks on which options are actually traded. An investor who does not want to devote the time and attention required to carry out this process can go to a dealer in equity derivatives and have a security custom-made to accomplish this or similar objectives, with considerably more flexibility in its design than the use of exchange-traded options.

HEDGING WITH OPTIONS: COSTS AND EXPECTATIONS

Based on the ground we have covered, we can now address the issue of defining the circumstances under which it is worthwhile to hedge with options, and when it is not.

Options provide a more flexible hedging vehicle than futures. As we saw, hedging with futures eliminates not only risk, but also opportunity of profit. Futures are therefore useful to eliminate the systemic risk that a whole group of stocks will fall in value, leaving the investor with the possibility that the specific stocks in the investor's portfolio will outperform or underperform the index. Only to that extent will the investor profit or lose.

Option hedging operates in the fashion of insurance, and coverage can be tailored to the investor's needs. The investor can insure him- or herself against the *systemic* risk that the whole market will crash by buying a put on the S&P 500. If the strike price of the put is substantially below the current market price (substantially out of the money), there is a large deductible, and the investor is protected only against a large fall. Or the investor can purchase a put with a strike price just below, or even above, the current market price to protect against any fall in the market, less the premium that was paid for purchasing the put option insurance. Alternatively, the investor can insure against the *specific* risk of loss in value of a particular stock by buying a put on that particular stock. In either case, the insurance involves paying a premium: the option premium. It can also involve a "deductible," equal to the extent, if any, to which the option is out of the money. The cost of this premium, and the deductible, must be weighed against the value of the insurance; that is, the consequences to the investor if the feared decline in value occurs.

If the investor suspects that there may be a big move in the market, but that the move might be either up or down, the insurance will be more valuable, since the cost of the premium is only a small part of the projected profits or losses. Since most investors think in exactly this way, options premiums tend to rise when large swings in market value are anticipated. Option *volatility* is the mathematical measure of this expectation. The greater the expected swings in market value, the higher the expected volatility and the higher the option premiums.

The investor's market expectations will determine whether the cost of a particular hedge is worthwhile. Suppose the S&P 500 is at 550 and a put option with three months left before its expiration date and with an exercise price of $550 is selling for 15. At $50 a point times 15 points, this means the put option costs $7,500. The exercise price of 550 is exactly equal to the current market price of the S&P index, so this option is *at* the money (rather than *in* or *out* of the money). As with an in-the-money option, the option has no intrinsic value, there is no deductible, and the price of the option is entirely composed of time premium.

This option premium of 15 points is approximately 3 percent of the market price of 550 (15 divided by 550 equals 3 percent.) Since this time premium is being paid for a three-month period (a quarter of a year), its cost is roughly 12 percent per year (4 quarters times 3 percent equals 12 percent). Suppose the investor has determined that, over many years, the average rate of return on a stock portfolio is approximately 10 percent a year. Paying a 12 percent insurance premium is therefore more than the entire expected 10 percent return on the portfolio. Since the investor expects the cost of the insurance to exceed the return on the investment, the insurance is too expensive and the investor is better off leaving the investment uninsured, or not making the investment at all.

If, however, the investor expects the market to rise or fall by 10 percent over the next three months, the purchase of the option does make sense. A 10 percent increase over three months less the 3 percent cost of the option would yield a 7 percent profit. If instead, the market declines by 10 percent over the next three months, the option purchase will reduce the loss from 10 percent to 3 percent (the 10 percent return on the option position less the 3 percent time premium paid for the option), so that the loss is reduced by 70 percent. Purchase of options makes the most sense when the investor believes the chances of the rise or fall in the price of stocks during the option period will much more than offset the option premium. Since option premiums tend to rise when price volatility is expected to be high, the actual market price of the option premium, reflecting general market expectations, must always be compared with the investor's own expectation of the volatility of the market during the option period.

DYNAMIC HEDGING

As we have seen, hedging involves costs just as any insurance does. If options are used to hedge, the cost is a time premium, which can be expressed as a percentage of the asset being hedged and which can be substantial in relation to the expected profits on that asset. This time premium can be reduced by selecting a strike price for the option below the current market price of the asset being hedged, but to the extent this is done, the self-insured "deductible" increases, limiting the protection in the event that there is a loss on the hedged asset. If hedging is done with futures or synthetic futures both the deductible and the time premium can be eliminated, so that the transaction costs are a very small percentage of the asset being hedged. However, use of futures or synthetic futures as a hedge eliminates the possibility of gain as well as the risk of loss; so the effect of the transaction may not be much different from selling the asset.

In many cases, a cost-effective hedge may also be imperfect. If the futures contract is somewhat different from the asset being hedged, as in the case of S&P 500 futures being used to hedge a stock portfolio that consists of a mix of stocks somewhat different than the S&P 500, then there remains a potential for gain or loss to the extent that the performance of the hedged asset differs from that of the hedge. The portfolio will gain or lose only to the extent that the stocks it contains both outperform or underperform those of the S&P 500. As previously discussed, this may be desired in certain cases.

Because of these costs and limitations of hedging, many assets are left unhedged most of the time. Both business executives and portfolio managers run many risks. As in day-to-day life, not every risk is insured. In the past, insuring against many risks was impossible: Traditional insurance was unavailable, and insurance in the form of options and futures contracts was available only on a very limited list of assets. Now, with bankers and derivative dealers offering new customized options, futures, and swaps contracts, insurance is usually available in the form of derivative hedges—but its use requires careful thought. The proposed hedge must be examined to see whether its time premium, deductible, limitations on profitability on the underlying asset, and any risks associated with steps incorporated in the transaction to reduce the cost of the hedge, such as sale of an option, are justified in light of the risks and expected returns of the underlying asset and the risk tolerance of the user of the hedge.

Often this analysis leads to the conclusion that hedging a single asset or a portfolio is appropriate at certain times, but not others. If hedging is appropriate, the hedge may need to be adjusted periodically as stock price and time to expiration change. This conclusion can lead to a strategy of *dynamic hedging,* in which the nature and extent of the hedge changes, depending on price movements, changes in the investor's expectation of future market conditions, and changes in the cost of the hedge. All three elements of the decision are continually changing.

Observations and assumptions about the price behavior of the option in relation to the price behavior of the underlying contract comprise the major inputs to the models, but the mathematical modeling of expected price behavior and fair value of various options can become very complex. For example, buying the right number of options at a given strike price to offset an anticipated 1-point move the next day in an underlying index or contract is not a simple matter.

Predictions must be made not only about the decline of the option's value with time, but its decline or increase as its distance from the strike price increases or decreases. Options tend to lose time value more rapidly as they approach expiration. Options also lose time value as the market moves away from the strike price. Finally, the option price changes depending upon the volatility of the underlying assets. All of these factors interrelate.

In dynamic hedging, these relationships may all be mathematically modeled. A calculation is made of the volatility and fair values implied by the current market price of the underlying index or contract itself and of the market price of each of the options currently being traded on that index or contract, each option varying from the others in terms of strike price and expiration date. The implied volatility calculated in this way is compared to the historical volatility of the index or contract and to the investor's own view of its likely future volatility, so that the investor can reach a conclusion whether current pricing is overpriced or a bargain. Likewise, the calculated fair value of each option traded can be compared to its actual market price to determine the attractiveness of the pricing of that particular option. The accuracy of the mathematical models used and the investor's market expectations will determine the successfulness of the decisions made.

PROGRAM TRADING

Another approach to the control of risk is that of *program trading*, under which many stocks in a portfolio may be bought or sold as predetermined price levels are reached. For example, this may involve a decision to sell if losses become too great, with the intention of waiting for a more promising point at which to reenter the market. If many market participants reach a decision to sell out at the same price level, the result can become a panic as everyone tries to sell at once, driving prices down to extremes. Analysts of the October 1987 crash in stock prices have suggested that this is exactly what happened at that time. In response, regulators have imposed limits on program trading, prohibiting it for a period of time when the Dow Jones average has declined a specified number of points. These limitations make market disruption less likely, but also limit the usefulness of program trading in those circumstances when it may be most needed by those who rely on it to protect them from risk. Use of options, futures, and swaps provides more certain protection to the investor than program trading and may also limit the risk to the system that program trading will drive prices to unrealistic levels.

SWAPS AND PRIVATELY WRITTEN OPTIONS AS ALTERNATIVES

The discussion of this chapter has focused principally on the use of publicly traded options for hedging purposes. For many stocks, there are no publicly traded options, and index options provide only an imperfect alternative. In these cases, the same objectives can be achieved through options negotiated privately with a derivative dealer or through swaps. Often, swaps include within themselves "embedded options" and forwards, so that the swap can be analyzed by breaking out each component option or for-

ward element. Terms and pricing of these instruments are nego-
tiable, making them more flexible vehicles than exchange-traded
options.

For example, the return on the previously discussed Philip
Morris stock could simply be swapped for the return on a com-
monly quoted interest rate instrument, such as Treasury bills. This
would be similar to selling the stock and using the proceeds to
buy Treasury bills. If the investor later decided that he or she
would prefer a stock market investment to a Treasury bill investment, the Treasury bill swap might then be traded for another
swap, exchanging the Treasury bill rate for the return on the S&P
500, for example. The net result would be equivalent to selling the
Philip Morris stock, investing the proceeds in Treasury bills, and
then selling the Treasury bills and buying a mutual fund composed of the stocks in the S&P 500 index.

Or a derivative dealer might write a collar for the Philip Morris stock, protecting the owner from any price decline below a predetermined level (the floor) by buying a put and offsetting the cost
of this put arrangement by taking from the owner any profit on
Philip Morris stock above another predetermined level (the cap).
This private arrangement is equivalent to buying a put and selling
a call in the public market (described in figure 6.4). The stock and
collar combination could then serve as collateral for borrowing to
make other investments, although regulations might restrict the
kind of investments that can be made in this situation.

The practicality of even these private arrangements depends
on the ability of the derivative dealer to hedge its exposure by the
use of options in the public markets, or at least by borrowing the
stock to permit short selling. For many stocks, there are no options
publicly traded, but the stock can be borrowed, so private contracts can be arranged at reasonable prices. If there are no options
on the stock, and the stock can't be borrowed, the derivative
dealer must then try to find a counterparty who wants to take the
opposite risk on the swap—sometimes a difficult task—or the
derivative dealer must try to calculate overall exposure and hedge
it in a portfolio-wide basis—a step imposing additional risks, and
therefore additional costs.

7

Business Risk Management

The essence of business is risk taking. Nothing ventured, nothing gained. However, this does not imply in any way that a business must take all the risks inherent in its enterprise. Generally speaking, a business or its managers should take only those risks that they set out to take as part of their enterprise, and eliminate or hedge all other risks. Figure 7.1 shows one simple way to visualize business risks.

BUSINESS RISKS

Primary Risks

Primary risks are those risks that must unavoidably be accepted as part of the decision to enter a particular line of business. They are the key to being in that business. To hedge or eliminate these risks would be the same as deciding to go out of business. Consider the following example: A businessman decides to pursue the business of buying wheat at harvesttime, storing it, and later selling it. The variation in the price of wheat during the course of the

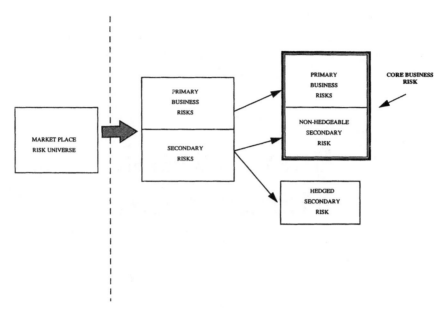

Figure 7.1 Business risks.

year, from harvesttime to final sale, constitutes an unavoidable primary risk, which cannot be avoided without eliminating the potential profit from the business as well. To eliminate all this price risk through some form of hedge constitutes a decision to get out of this business. Or perhaps our businessman decides to get into a different business, such as the wheat distribution business. In this case, price risk is no longer an unavoidable primary risk and could be hedged away, but there is a different primary risk. A distribution business would involve investing money to create a network of stores for distribution, and this unavoidably entails the risk that these stores would fail to be profitable.

Although hedging away the entire primary risk is tantamount to exiting the business, the businessman in the preceding example can still decide to *moderate* his primary risk profile. For example, he might decide to sign an agreement with another company, perhaps one with a larger capital base, under which he can sell a portion of his wheat to the company at a floor price regardless of market prices. By doing so the businessman has not hedged away his entire primary risks, but has mitigated the effect of a disastrous fall in market prices.

There are two important points to remember about primary risks. First, for most business enterprises, primary risks constitute a complex package of risks and cannot be isolated as easily as in the example. Second, the package of primary risks is constantly changing; or more correctly, *should be* constantly changing as the managers of the business shift strategies and tactics try to adapt or take advantage of a competitive business environment. A business with a static package of primary risks may eventually stagnate and atrophy unless, of course, it has a product or technology that no one else can replicate and whose demand is eternally constant or even growing. For most businesses this is a utopian dream.

Secondary Risks

Secondary risks are the risks that come with a business along with the package of primary risks. These are risks that the business does not want to take and therefore should be eliminated or hedged to the extent this is practical.

Some secondary risks can be entirely eliminated through financial derivatives or other instruments; others can only be eliminated by entering into private contracts with other businesses, suppliers, or customers. Still others cannot be entirely eliminated at reasonable expense and can only be mitigated in an approximate manner. The remaining risks must simply be accepted as part of the business. The primary risks of a business along with non-hedgeable secondary risks constitute the core risk package of the business.

For examples of these different types of risks, let us return to our wheat dealer. If our businessman decides he does not want to face the risks of the changing prices of wheat, and he decides to go into the wheat distribution business, the price of wheat becomes a secondary risk which he will probably want to hedge. As described in earlier chapters, there is a large public market in grain and other agricultural futures. For a reasonable price, this grain distributor can buy wheat futures or put options to fully protect himself against the risk of decline in the price of wheat. Of course, he is not forced to fully hedge against this risk; he may simply want to protect himself against a disastrous price change by hedging part of his estimated exposure to these price changes—for example, by buying a small amount of futures, or buying put options that are far out of the money. In such cases, he will be accepting some degree of price risk exposure as part of his package of core risks. But if he wants to, he can entirely eliminate the risk of wheat price changes. Not only is this a fully hedgeable secondary risk, but it is a risk that can be hedged simply by turning to the public futures and options markets.

As another example, suppose you are running a business making tennis shoes in the People's Republic of China and selling them in the United States. One secondary risk is the cost of shipping finished goods from the People's Republic of China to the United States. This cost can be isolated and separated. You can decide to eliminate the risk that this cost will fluctuate widely by signing a long-term shipping contract fixing the shipping costs over a period of several years. This type of contract is fairly common and will entirely eliminate the risk of increased shipping costs for the duration of the contract.

Note that in neither of these cases are *all* risks truly eliminated by the hedge. In private contracts, there is always the risk that the counterparty may default. Users of derivative contracts may also face a similar risk, other legal risks, and more subtle risks such as *basis risk,* which is the risk that the price of the futures contract will not fully converge with that of the cash market. While legal risks are often difficult to hedge, an entire market has actually developed for hedging basis risk. Subject to these unavoidable credit and legal uncertainties, which are perhaps part of the core risk of business, it is still correct that the specific risks of price changes or changes in shipping costs have been entirely hedged.

As another example of a risk that cannot be entirely eliminated, imagine you are a pension fund manager and have decided that you would like to take advantage of investment opportunities presented by the stock markets outside the United States. Your analysis shows that there are a number of pharmaceutical stocks in France that are undervalued, and you decide to invest in a portfolio of these stocks. However, although you feel that this portfolio will improve its valuation in the near future, you are not sure about the value of the French franc relative to the U.S. dollar. This is a secondary risk, and, as we have seen, currency risks can be hedged through a foreign exchange swap. In this particular case, however, the risk cannot be hedged perfectly. Because the value of the stock portfolio itself is unpredictable, it is impossible to predict in advance the size of the forward currency contract required to hedge the risk. You cannot know at the outset how much the portfolio's value in French francs will go up or down over the investment period. You can only hedge in an approximate manner. If the pension fund manager decides to make this investment, he or she must accept some degree of foreign exchange exposure.

A similar, but less hedgeable, example is that of a portfolio of Brazilian stocks. Not only is it impossible to quantify the foreign exchange exposure exactly, but the quantified risk cannot be easily eliminated, because a long-term foreign exchange market does not exist for Brazilian currency at this time, in either the futures or forward markets. Unless the investor could find a private party willing to underwrite this risk, he or she would have to accept a substantial degree of exposure to foreign currency as part of the core risk in making the investment.

WHICH BUSINESS RISKS
SHOULD BE HEDGED?

Hedging away all the core risks inherent in a business proposition unavoidably involves hedging away all the profit opportunity as well. However, a business manager might well decide to *mitigate* or limit even the primary risks of the business. Even if this involves some limitation on potential profits, the businessperson may prefer to run the enterprise on the basis of moderate, rather than high, risk. Secondary risks, those that are not inherent to the business proposition, should be eliminated if it is practical to do so. Those secondary risks that are hedgeable can be isolated and entirely eliminated through a hedge in public or private derivatives markets or through a private contract. Those that cannot be isolated or hedged exactly should be hedged to the fullest extent possible.

The concept of secondary, nonhedgeable risk is something of a misnomer. If the risk cannot be eliminated, it should be acknowledged as part of the core risk of the venture. The investor who wishes to speculate on French pharmaceutical stocks, described earlier, must accept some degree of exchange rate risk as part of the core risks of the investment, even if he or she decides to limit it to the extent possible through a currency swap.

This evaluation does not take place in a vacuum: Eliminating risk has a cost. Eliminating secondary risks is not only a matter of deciding which risks the business wants to take, but which risks can be eliminated in a cost-effective manner. For example, if there is a secondary risk that can be eliminated through a contract with another business, the cost associated with the contract should be evaluated like any business decision. In the example of shoes manufactured in China and sold in the United States, the decision to eliminate the shipment-cost risk is the same as deciding whether you want to be in the shipping business narrowly defined. You should remain in this line of business only if you think you can carry it out in a profitable way. If you think it is more economical to eliminate this risk through a hedge or a private contract, you should not accept it as a core risk. A similar analysis applies to the decision to hedge a financial risk by using derivatives or any other means. The decision to accept or reject the risk as a core risk of the business should be based on whether taking that particular risk at that cost offers a profit opportunity or not.

Evaluating risk is a dynamic process. The package of core risks is continuously changing, and a business manager should continuously and rigorously test every risk to decide whether to eliminate it, hedge it, or accept it as part of the core risk of the business. The process of analyzing the risks in a business and identifying the core risk package should follow top-down and bottom-up methods simultaneously to achieve a balanced and consistent approach throughout the firm.

In the top-down method, senior management must decide on the core risk package of the overall business strategy. For example, one firm may decide that all exposure to commodity price movements should be fully hedged whenever possible. Another company, say a global conglomerate, may decide that global currency exposure arising out of its business is part of the company's core risk package and, therefore, should not be hedged, but carefully monitored and managed like any other line of business. In either case, such a broad policy should be clearly communicated throughout the firm and commodity exposure at any level of the firm's operations should be hedged.

The bottom-up method starts at a lower level in the organization. This could be at the departmental level or a divisional level or even, in a multinational organization, at a country level. For example, a particular division might prefer to hedge its currency exposures because currency fluctuations would have an enormous impact on its net earnings and because trading currency exposures is not within its core expertise. The management of the division should inform corporate headquarters about this and seek permission to hedge its exposures. If the corporation as a whole includes currency exposures in its core risk package, then the division should transfer responsibility for managing its currency exposures to the corporate treasury so that its own financial performance is insulated from the effects of the currency fluctuations.

The top-down and bottom-up approaches should be complementary and must be harmonized. Corporate management should have a clear idea of the core risk package and communicate it to the organization. At the business unit level, management should be able to adopt its own core risk package, depending upon its strategy and expertise. Discrepancies must be resolved either through mutual agreement to adjust strategic decisions or through the transfer of risk from the business unit level to the corporate treasury level. This allows the particular division to focus on its own core business risks, but in a way consistent with the overall business strategy of the corporation as a whole. It also keeps the corporation as a whole informed of the risks and expertise of its various divisions, so it can decide when and how to modify its core risks.

In summary, all risks that are not included in the core risk package of the business proposition should be eliminated or hedged. If they are not eliminated or hedged, for cost reasons or otherwise, then management is implicitly stating that they accept those risks as part of the core risk package of their enterprise, and each of those risks should be monitored and managed like any other line of business.

CAN BUSINESS RISKS BE HEDGED WITH DERIVATIVES?

Many business risks can be hedged with derivatives. These range from risks arising from specific, narrow transactions (such as the currency risk that is part of investing in foreign stocks) to broad strategic exposures which may be part of the core risk of the business (such as the risk of price changes in the earlier example of buying and selling wheat). Derivatives can be used to eliminate certain risks entirely or limit them to varying degrees and for varying periods of time. The following examples illustrate a range of applications of derivatives. In some of the examples several objectives, including the management of risk, are simultaneously met.

A Short-Term Hedge for Long-Term Financing

A large company on the Fortune 200 list, one of the global leaders in the high-technology manufacturing industry, has very little debt on its balance sheet. The company wants to raise $200 million of financing for capital expenditures and has decided to borrow the money in the public debt market. Due to the long-term nature of the projects, the company correctly decides to issue a 30-year bond at a fixed interest rate.

The interest paid on the 30-year financing will have a noticeable impact on the feasibility and success of the capital expenditure projects. The greater the interest, the greater the cost of financing and the narrower the profit margins. Indeed, if the interest rate is too high, the project might become too costly and risky. It is the month of August, and long-term interest rates are low. If the company completed the financing today, it would pay 8 percent per annum, which would be comfortably within the parameters established by the financial analysis of the projects.

However, the chief financial officer is concerned about the risk of interest rates rising in the near future. The company is not a frequent borrower and therefore does not have a shelf registration on file with the SEC, which would greatly shorten the process of obtaining necessary regulatory approval for a public offering and allow the company to come to the market quickly. Also, its internal approval procedures for financing are elaborate and would require a period of several months to complete. All told, the CFO estimates three months will be needed to obtain all the internal approvals and submit the required SEC filings. If interest rates rise substantially during this three-month period, it could threaten the viability of the projects. The company therefore decides to enter a derivatives transaction called a *Treasury rate guarantee* (TRG), a type of interest rate hedge.

A TRG allows a company that is issuing debt (the *Issuer*) to hedge the economics of the financing prior to completion. In this case, although the issuer's final interest cost will be determined at closing, an interest rate hedge can be structured to yield a one-time cash settlement that achieves the economic effect of closing the bond issue at today's rates. A TRG accomplishes this by hedging with Treasury securities whose value rises or falls with interest rate changes. An increase in the cost of financing is thus offset by an increase in the value of the hedge. (See figure 7.2.)

The execution of this hedge involves a series of customized contracts with a broker/dealer establishing the size and maturity of the underlying exposure to be hedged and the exact terms of the hedge. In this case, the underlying exposure is the cost of financing the $200 million, 30-year bond issue. The exact terms of the hedge would depend on the economics of the underlying Treasury market and the length of the hedge period. The terms of this contract are established at the outset, including the specific Treasury securities to be used and a specific settlement date for the contract.

When the hedge is unwound at the time the bond is issued, the issuer receives or makes a payment equal to the change in market value of the hedge. This payment closely approximates the change in present value of the cost of the financing resulting from a change in interest rates over the hedge period. If interest rates fall, the market value of the hedge will decrease. The issuer will make a payment to the dealer, but this payment will be offset by the reduced cost of financing due to the fall in interest rates. If interest rates rise, the market value of the hedge will rise. The cost of financing will increase, but the issuer will receive a payment from the dealer that will offset this new cost.

However, a TRG does not eliminate every risk. It does not hedge against changes in corporate credit spread risk—that is, the risk that the cost of financing will change due to changed per-

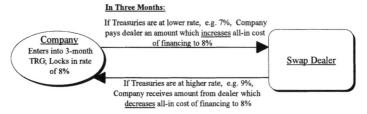

Figure 7.2   Treasury rate guarantee.

ceptions about the credit risk of the issuer. It is also possible the issuer will not be able to issue the bonds at all. For example, the issuer's finance committee might not approve the transaction or the issuer may meet with difficulties in making the required SEC filings. In this case, the unwinding of the hedge will result in a cash profit or loss to the business, not a hedge of a new financing. The hedge is also subject to basis risk. If the Treasuries used to implement the hedge differ from the Treasuries ultimately used to price the bonds, the hedge may not be closely matched to the financing, and the cash payment resulting from the hedge may not closely match the change in the cost of the financing due to interest rate fluctuations.

This type of transaction is straightforward, common, and very efficiently priced. The interest rate on the new bond issue will probably be based on Treasury interest rates, and the Treasury market is very liquid. It is therefore possible to price the hedge efficiently. The cost of the hedge is generally a small and reasonable price to pay to lock in an interest rate for a complicated financial transaction before proceeding with all the costs, commitments, and expectations involved in bringing the bond issue to completion. The risk that the bond issue will never be completed and that the transaction will therefore give rise to a profit or loss unrelated to the project is small in relation to the other considerations involved. This is a Wall Street version of the locked-in rate on home mortgages many banks are beginning to provide to home buyers, who are then free to shop for a house without the fear that a rise in interest rates might limit their ability to buy the house they choose.

Exploiting Comparative Advantages: Asset Liability Currency Mismatch

A Scandinavian shipping company's main business is running cruise ships between the United States and Caribbean Islands. It therefore has large revenue flows in U.S. dollars. The company is planning to buy two new ships and is considering buying the ships from a builder in the United Kingdom. The shipbuilding company produces very fine ships and has a strong international reputation. However, the main reason the shipping company is considering giving the order to the U.K. company is the availability of a very competitive loan package from the U.K. EXIM bank. (Most countries have some form of government-subsidized export-import banks, known as *EXIM banks,* which specialize in financing that country's international trade.) The full purchase price of the ships is about £50 million, which at current foreign exchange rates would be equivalent to U.S.$75 million. The U.K. EXIM bank has agreed to provide a loan for the full purchase price of the ships. The loan will amortize over 10 years; that is, the principal is fully repaid in installments, along with the interest, over a 10-year period. The loan will be denominated in sterling and the interest rate will be set at 8 percent per annum. The offer from the EXIM bank is particularly attractive because the interest rate on such a loan obtained in the open market would be about 9 percent per annum.

The company wants to take advantage of the 1 percent interest savings on the £50 million ($75 million) it needs to borrow. However, it is not comfortable with the long-term currency mismatch between its liability payments in sterling and its revenue inflows in U.S. dollars. In order to eliminate this mismatch the company enters into a 10-year currency swap to convert its sterling liability to a 10-year U.S. dollar liability.

In this swap, the company would receive 8 percent in sterling on its loan amount of £50 million. In return, the company will pay the swap dealer U.S. LIBOR on the dollar equivalent amount (i.e., $75 million). This would effectively allow the company to use the sterling it receives in the swap to pay interest and principal on the EXIM loan while utilizing its U.S. dollar asset (the shipping business) as a source of the U.S. dollars it pays on the swap. Since the EXIM loan amortizes over time, the notional amount of the swap would be structured to replicate the amortizing notional amounts. The company would use the sterling received as the swap amortized to pay off the corresponding amortization amount on the loan. (See figure 7.3.)

In order to match its liability in sterling (the loan) with its asset in U.S. dollars (revenues from its shipping) the company has entered into a currency swap that converts sterling cash outflows on the loan to U.S. dollar cash outflows. By doing so, the company has eliminated the mismatch between currency flows and at the same time availed itself of the subsidized financing provided by the EXIM bank.

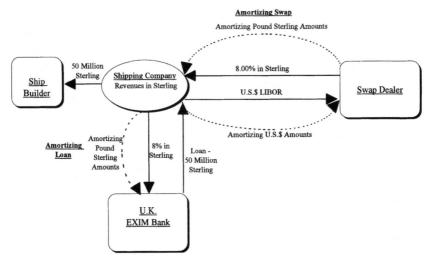

Figure 7.3 Amortizing currency swap.

Price Risk of Restricted Stock Holding

US-Corp is a privately owned software company that has received an offer from a French company (F-Corp) to buy all its European operations for $200 million. The offer is a part cash, part stock offer, with 75 percent of the purchase price to be paid in F-Corp shares. However, the F-Corp shares provided as part of the purchase price would have some selling restrictions attached for a period of several years following the sale. These restrictions are fairly common in stock acquisitions when one party does not wish to create selling pressure on its stock—especially if it is planning other acquisitions. The partners who own US-Corp think that the offer is a good one and would like to accept it. But they are not comfortable holding $150 million in restricted stock of F-Corp and would rather have the money invested in a diversified portfolio of European stocks. In order to transform their illiquid holding in the stock of one French company into a diversified portfolio of European stock, the partners decide to enter into a one-year equity swap.

Under the equity swap, US-Corp would pay the swap counterparty all the dividends received on the U.S.$150M market value of F-Corp stock plus the price change on the F-Corp stock between the start and end of the swap. US-Corp would receive from the swap counterparty the change in the value of a European stock index (inclusive of dividends) between the start and end of the swap. (See figure 7.4.) During the period of the swap US-Corp eliminates most of its exposure to price changes of F-Corp's stock. (Broker/dealers may sometimes have a holding period restriction before they would enter into such a transaction.)

Asset-based Financing

ABC is a large conglomerate, and one of its subsidiary units is among the largest producers of gold in the world. ABC has developed a plan to diversify into the construction equipment manufacturing business by acquiring a large stake in a fast-growing company in that industry. After long and extensive negotiations, it has reached the conclusion that its target company can be acquired through a cash offer of $500 million. But ABC is not cash rich, and its management does not wish to raise the $500 million through further borrowing—which would add leverage to its balance sheet. Moreover, the company needs dollars for the acquisition, but its base of operations is located in a country that imposes certain exchange controls. After spending a month analyzing various alternatives, the company decides to finance its acquisition by using part of the future production of gold from its mines. The company accomplishes this by setting up a special-purpose financing vehicle with gold-based financing. (See figure 7.5.)

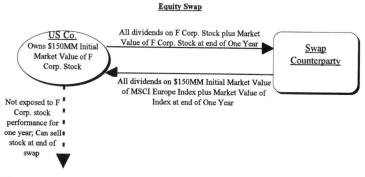

Figure 7.4   Equity swap.

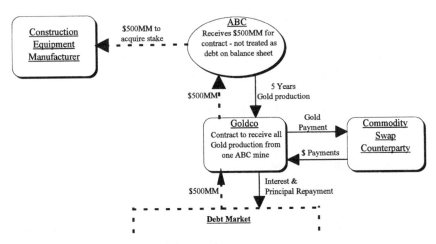

Figure 7.5   Asset-based financing.

Under this plan, ABC sets up a separate corporate entity, Goldco, and enters into a contract giving Goldco the right to the entire production from one of its mines. With this asset as security, Goldco enters the debt market and borrows funds in dollars, which are then paid to ABC in return for the contract, giving it the right to the production for one of its mines. Because ABC is not liable for the debt but has merely agreed to produce and deliver the gold that Goldco has used to secure the debt, this debt appears only on the books of Goldco, and not on those of ABC. The lenders, however, are still reasonably sure of repayment of the debt, based on the past performance and the expected output of the mine.

With a further modification to the structure of this transaction, the borrowing can be separated from the risks inherent in the fluctuation of the price of gold. The purchasers of the bond need not be at risk on the price of gold. Goldco enters into a commodity swap whereby it delivers a predetermined amount of gold to the counterparty in exchange for dollar payments which exactly match its interest and principal payments to its bondholders. ABC thus meets its financing needs in the currency it needs, without adding leverage to its balance sheet. At the same time it has hedged its risk due to fluctuations in the price of gold over the term of the financing.

CONCLUSION

The examples presented in this chapter illustrate the use of derivative transactions to hedge business risks. They range from narrow transaction hedges to broad strategic risk management.

They show that there is a broad range of corporate risks that can be hedged or mitigated using derivatives. Senior management, directors, and other supervisors must constantly review the package of risks to which a business is exposed and must decide in an unequivocal manner which risks comprise the core risk package to be accepted and managed as part of the business, and which risks represent secondary risks. Secondary risks should be eliminated through contractual arrangements with other businesses, or should be hedged. Many of these secondary risks can be hedged through the use of derivatives or derivatives-based structured transactions. However, if a secondary risk cannot be hedged through a derivative or a private contract, it should be accepted as one of the core risks of the business venture and managed accordingly.

8

Investing Through Derivatives

Any investment involves two basic decisions. The first and primary decision is selection of the asset in which to invest. No investment should be made before the investor thoroughly understands the asset class and the asset itself. The second, and often equally important, decision is the selection of the amount of leverage to use in the investment. That is, the investor must decide whether to borrow the entire sum to be invested, to borrow nothing and invest only his or her own money, or to do something in between.

These questions are just as pertinent when investing using derivatives as when making any other investments. In fact, they are precursors to a decision to use derivatives. If the answer to the first question is that a particular asset or asset class does not have characteristics that are suitable to the investment goals, then it is unnecessary even to consider the use of derivatives. However, the risks and rewards of an asset may be modified using derivatives. An investor may wish to invest in an asset class that he or she would otherwise avoid if the investment is modified so as to meet the investor's requirements through the use of derivatives.

After the decision to invest in a particular asset has been made and the appropriate level of leverage has been selected, you can again address the issue of whether to use derivatives to make the investment. The decision is often fairly straightforward. In general, derivatives should be used when they enable investment in an asset class that might not otherwise be readily accessible to the investor or when they make the process of investment in a particular asset more efficient. Derivatives could also be used in investing if they enable the investor to incorporate the desired leverage in the most efficient or most convenient manner. Finally, derivatives or structured transactions can be used to create an investment within an asset class tailored to meet specific risk/return objectives. Of course, in many instances the reasons for using derivatives will include elements of more than one of these considerations.

The examples that follow illustrate a range of investments using structured derivative transactions. Each of these investments fulfills at least one of the preceding requirements.

USING DERIVATIVES TO INVEST IN INTEREST RATES

GBF is a global bond fund that invests in government bonds issued by the major industrialized countries. GBF uses moderate leverage in its investment strategy. It does not have counterparty credit lines with derivatives dealers at this time and has decided not to invest in the infrastructure needed to manage a portfolio of swaps. However, GBF has identified a special investment opportunity in the French bond market. The fund manager feels that the yield curve in the French government bond market is currently extremely steep and should flatten somewhat during the next year to more normal levels. For example, interest rates for short-term bonds seem low at 5 percent, while rates for long-term bonds seem relatively high at 8 percent. GBF could buy a structured note tailored to reflect its investment perspective.

Figure 8.1 illustrates the concept behind this transaction. The current spread between 3-month and 10-year French interest rates is 3 percent. The fund manager believes that over the coming year this spread will revert to a more normal level of 2 percent. To achieve the objective, the fund manager needs to make an investment equivalent to buying 10-year bonds and selling

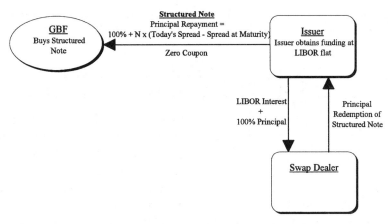

Figure 8.1   Yield curve spread note.

short the 3-month bills, and maintain this position over the coming year.

By using a structured note, GBF not only can easily make this
investment, it can add whatever degree of leverage it wishes, and
can make the investment denominated in terms of U.S. dollars,
without exposure in fluctuations in the value of the French franc if
the fund so desires. The note would offer GBF a leveraged play on
the spread between 10-year and 3-month French franc interest rates.

The principal repayment on the note would be as follows:

$$N \times \text{(today's spread} - \text{spread at maturity)}$$

where *spread* equals the interest rate on a 10-year French government bond less the interest rate on a 3-month French government
bond; but if this figure would be negative, spread is equal to zero.
If the GBF fund manager is correct and the yield curve does flatten, spread at maturity will be less than today's spread. Therefore,
the principal repayment of the note would be correspondingly
high, and GBF would have earned an above-market rate of return
for one year.

GBF is, of course, exposed to a further steepening of the yield
curve. In such a situation GBF would earn a below-market rate of
return.

As is typical in such transactions, the issuer has hedged all its
exposure due to the redemption formula by entering into an offset-

ting contract with a dealer. The net result for the issuer is a straight dollar financing at a cost lower than its normal funding cost.

SYNTHETIC BONDS IN FOREIGN CURRENCIES: CREDIT RATING ARBITRAGE

USIC is a U.S. insurance company that is predominantly in the life and property casualty insurance business. It has a large book of business originating in Japan and therefore a long-duration liability exposure in Japanese yen, as it may be required to pay insurance claims in Japanese yen far in the future. In order to cover this liability USIC would like to buy long-duration yen bonds. In order to match its liabilities, USIC needs at least a 4 percent rate of interest on its assets. However, Japanese yen interest rates are currently at an extremely low level. Single-A-rated yen bonds are trading in the market at about 3¼ percent interest rate in yen. USIC will not, as a matter of policy, invest in credits that are rated lower than single-A by the rating agencies. USIC met its objectives by doing a structured private placement investment.

USIC's investment bank informs USIC that ECU (European currency units)-denominated bonds issued by the Republic of Italy are trading cheap relative to comparably rated bonds in the market, due to the uncertain political and economic environment in Italy. However, the credit rating agencies are maintaining a positive outlook on Italy and its ability to meet its debt obligations, and the bonds are still rated single-A. USIC's investment bank therefore recommends that USIC buy the Italy bonds asset swapped to yen. That is, they recommend that USIC buy the Italian bonds and swap all the ECU payments from the bonds into yen through a currency swap. The currency swap would replace all the ECU cash flows from the underlying ECU bonds with yen cash flows and create a synthetic yen bond with a yield of 4.25 percent and a single-A credit rating. (See figure 8.2.)

CREATING A DIVERSIFIED PORTFOLIO USING EQUITY SWAPS

CPF is a corporate pension fund managing about $20 billion of assets. During the last three years it has increased its investments

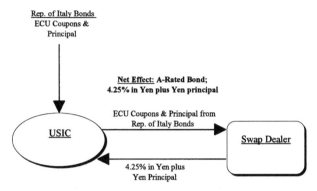

Figure 8.2   Credit arbitrage note.

in European equities considerably in order to diversify its portfolio. CPF does not have the expertise or information base to analyze individual European stocks very well and therefore has expended a great deal of time and money using European equity investment managers. CPF has reached the conclusion that its objective is to invest in a broad portfolio of European stocks, that is, to make a sector investment in the European equity market. It would therefore like to create a diversified portfolio that would match the returns on the market as a whole, adopting a passive, indexed investment strategy, rather than trying to locate and monitor effective active managers.

CPF can enter into a total return swap in which it pays a floating rate, such as LIBOR plus a spread, and receives the total return on a broad European equity index or a combination of specific European stock indices. This equity swap lets it receive the return on the European equity index without actually purchasing each of the underlying stocks that make up the index. In effect, the equity swap is a convenient means of investing in the broad European equity market, which can be employed without leverage or with as much leverage as desired. It efficiently permits CPF to match the return on the market as a whole. In order to meet its floating value payments, CPF will invest its funds in bank CDs that pay interest at LIBOR. The swap negates the need for hiring European equity investment managers and dealing with the commissions, fees, delivery, and custody issues of actu-

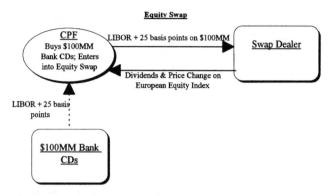

Figure 8.3   Structured swap—equity index.

ally owning such stocks. It is similar to a customized version of an S&P 500 futures contract in the United States.

Terms of the swap are as follows:

Notional amount	$100 million
Term	1 year
CPF pays	3-month LIBOR + 25 basis points
CPF receives	Total return on the General European Equity Index (calculated as $100 million × index at end of year ÷ index at start of year + any dividends paid on index stocks)

For example, if the index appreciates by 10 percent in the year, CPF will receive a payment of $10 million (equal to 10 percent of $100 million) plus whatever dividends were paid. Similarly, if the index declines by 10 percent, CPF will owe $10 million. In each case, CPF must pay an amount equal to the LIBOR + 25 basis points. (See figure 8.3.)

INVESTING IN FIXED INCOME EMERGING MARKETS

EMF is an emerging market fund based in Bermuda. It invests in debt securities issued by emerging market countries around the world. A large proportion of its portfolio is invested in Latin American countries. During the past few weeks, the fund managers have noticed an anomaly in the market prices of two securities issued by Argentina. The trading price difference between Argentina par bonds (fixed rate) due March 31, 2023 (ARG) and Argentina floating rate bonds due March 31, 2005 (FRBs) has historically been around 20 percent, with the FRBs on top. However, the current price difference is approximately 4 percent. The prices of both have dropped, but the FRBs have dropped more dramatically. EMF believes that the price spread will widen to normal levels within the next year. Therefore, EMF would like to create a synthetic asset position that would be profitable if their view of the price spread proves correct. EMF enters into a price-spread swap transaction to create such a synthetic asset.

In this price-spread swap transaction, EMF synthetically goes long Argentina FRBs and short ARGs for six months through a total return swap. On the maturity date of the swap, EMF receives a payment based on the difference between the FRBs and the ARGs and pays a fixed amount, which is defined at the outset of the swap. EMF achieves higher returns as the price spread between FRBs and ARGs (defined as FRB minus ARG) widens. On the other hand, if the price spread narrows or goes negative EMF would pay an amount to the dealer in addition to the fixed amount described above. EMF would then pay an amount to the dealer in addition to the fixed percent stated at the beginning of the transaction. For example, EMF enters into a 6-month Argentina FRB versus Argentina pars price-spread swap with the following terms:

Notional amount	$10 million
Settlement date	March 1995
Maturity date	Six months from settlement date

Settlement Payments on the Maturity Date.
(See figure 8.4.)

- EMF pays 4½% of the notional amount to dealer.
- EMF receives (FRB − ARG) × 100% of the notional amount.

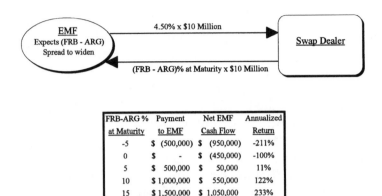

FRB-ARG % at Maturity	Payment to EMF	Net EMF Cash Flow	Annualized Return
-5	$ (500,000)	$ (950,000)	-211%
0	$ -	$ (450,000)	-100%
5	$ 500,000	$ 50,000	11%
10	$ 1,000,000	$ 550,000	122%
15	$ 1,500,000	$ 1,050,000	233%

Figure 8.4   Structured investment—emerging market debt.

- If (FRB – ARG) is negative then EMF pays dealer (ARG – FRB) × 100% of the notional amount.

USING DERIVATIVES TO PUSH THE LIMITS OF FIDUCIARY RESTRAINTS

MMF is a short-term money market fund that invests only in U.S. government or government agency securities. Its investment objective is to produce floating rate returns at LIBOR plus a spread while protecting the principal invested. The money market fund arena is highly competitive. In order to attract more investors, MMF needs to manage its investments aggressively to earn as high a spread over LIBOR as possible without violating the constraints incorporated in the fund's policy and guidelines, which specifically permit investments in AAA-rated bonds only. MMF has received a proposal for a structured note issued by a U.S. government agency, which would earn a return of LIBOR + 200, an extremely large spread compared to what EMF has seen in the market place.

This particular note is a government agency security that pays a coupon of LIBOR plus 200 basis points every three months so long as the U.S. dollar–Japanese yen currency exchange rate remains within the narrow band of 102 to 107 yen per dollar. If the exchange rate moves out of this band, the coupon quickly drops to zero. In fact, if the exchange rate moves too far out of the band,

MMF is in danger of losing principal value, because the principal repayment at maturity would be less than par. (See figure 8.5.)

Most of the MMF's other assets are government agency notes that pay a coupon of LIBOR plus a small spread until maturity and then pay back the full principal amount at maturity. By investing in these securities, MMF is only taking credit exposure to the government agencies. Because of the triple-A rating that government agencies receive, the additional spread that MMF receives above LIBOR is small.

The U.S. dollar–Japanese yen exchange-rate-linked note that MMF is considering contains the same amount of credit risk as the more traditional agency paper that MMF holds. However, this note contains a substantially different type of market risk, magnified by leverage, which produces the potentially higher returns when compared to the more traditional investments. Although each of these investments involves government agency notes, and they are similar in that respect, they involve entirely different risk profiles.

By investing in the structured notes, MMF is taking a market view that the U.S. dollar/Japanese yen exchange rate will remain very stable over the life of the note. Additionally, in order to

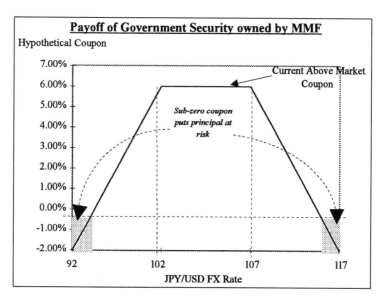

Figure 8.5   Exchange-rate-linked note.

obtain such a large spread over LIBOR, this note employs a substantial amount of leverage. If MMF invests in this note and turns out to be correct about the stability of the exchange rate, the overall performance of its portfolio will be enhanced. However, if MMF is wrong, and the exchange rate moves out of the narrow band, the amount of leverage employed could be disastrous to MMF's returns. Not only would MMF receive a coupon rate of zero, but it also might not receive its full principal amount at maturity.

This example illustrates the need for caution by modern corporations and investment funds to ensure that their internal guidelines and external disclosures reflect changing alternatives offered by the marketplace. Notes issued by U.S. government agencies are traditionally considered safe and secure investments from a credit risk standpoint. Many guidelines and state statutes specifically permit such investments by investment funds for exactly this reason. However, when these U.S. government agencies issue products such as structured notes involving terms that create high levels of market risk, someone must analyze the risk and reward characteristics of the investment and not simply assume that because the note has been issued by a government agency it is a safe and conservative investment. The decision whether or not a particular investment risk is suitable should be based not only on credit risk, but also on market volatility risks of the investment.

CONCLUSION

As these examples show, derivatives can be used to create an almost infinite range of investment products, and of embedded leverage levels. These products can be useful to enable investment in sectors or asset types that cannot be readily or efficiently accessed through cash markets. Whether they are appropriate investments should be determined on the basis of two fundamental factors which are, in fact, the relevant considerations for any investments. First, do the asset class and particular asset have characteristics that meet the investor's needs? Second, how much leverage is embedded in the investment, and how much should this be increased or decreased to meet the investor's risk/reward profile for this particular investment, as part of the investor's portfolio? If a certain asset or level of leverage is not appropriate, then the use of derivatives will not make it appropriate, but derivatives can often be used to adjust the leverage or even modify the characteristics of the asset so that both are appropriate.

Part 3

UNDERSTANDING AND MANAGING RISK

INTRODUCTION

As Aristotle's story of Thales demonstrates, derivatives are hardly a new invention. Nor is their popularity new. The agricultural commodity exchanges in the United States have long been a commonplace financial tool used by growers and processors to hedge their business risks, and by speculators seeking profits, by in effect writing insurance against those business risks. Derivatives are now being used more than ever, by a wider variety of users and for a wider number of purposes. Most recently, certain users of derivatives have been blamed for large losses and have been the subject of correspondingly large lawsuits. In the last two years, one of the world's oldest investment banks and one of the wealthiest U.S. counties have failed, and much of the blame has been placed on derivatives. Some state legislatures have proposed banning derivatives entirely, and Congress, the SEC, the CFTC, and the Federal Reserve have proposed and debated more limited remedies. Small and large investors are increasingly warned to check for derivatives before making investments, as if they were some kind of infectious disease.

While the losses have been large and well publicized, they have involved only a very small percentage of the value of the derivatives that exist today in the world's financial market. It is abundantly clear that derivatives are now a pervasive presence in the modern business and investing world. Some take comfort from the fact that so small a percentage of derivative uses has gone amiss. Others worry that all derivatives will fail, taking the world economy with them. Everyone considers disaster scenarios from time to time, even if only in the middle of a sleepless night. Not all such concerns are groundless. Dinosaurs dominated the earth for millions of years; then they suddenly disappeared. A little closer to home, every major stock exchange in the world faced destruction at some time during this century, except in the United States—and even the stocks on the New York Stock Exchange lost more than half their value during the great depression. Two world wars overshadowed the European stock exchanges for a time. Revolution destroyed the stock exchange of China. War, revolution, expropriations, devaluation, panic, and other human and natural events have wreaked financial havoc from time to time. In the course of life on this planet, death and taxes are said to be the only certainties.

Given the fragility of the human condition, it would be foolish to dismiss out of hand the possibility that the $30 trillion structure of newly created derivatives, which are now such an integral part of world finance, could collapse. Even without derivatives, the world's financial and even governmental structures could collapse. They have done so before. But the important question is how to deal with life as we know it. In the next four chapters, therefore, we will focus on how directors, pension fiduciaries, and other decision makers can successfully carry out their duties in a world where derivatives exist and disaster is lurking, with or without derivatives. It is beyond the scope of our present work to provide a prescription for restructuring the world's financial system to eliminate the risk associated with derivatives. Nevertheless, before turning to the issues that confront individual decision makers, some discussion of the place of derivatives in the world's financial structure is in order.

9

Summary of Risk

Measuring the presence and risk of derivatives is not easy, considering how many varieties there are. Assessing the overall systemic risk posed by derivatives is even more complicated. First, the total volume of derivatives is not a good measure of the risk exposure represented by derivatives. In many cases, derivatives actually reduce risk, and distinguishing between hedges and speculation is increasingly subtle in modern financial transactions. Second, it is inaccurate to attribute to derivatives every disaster *involving* derivatives. Most of such disasters are the result of shortcomings that have caused disasters time and again, independent of derivatives. These shortcomings include lack of internal controls, inadequate management attention, too much leverage, bad business judgment, or simply the inevitable fact that when business risks are taken, there will sometimes be business losses. Even good businesspeople sometimes suffer losses—if they didn't they wouldn't be in business. A good businessperson or investor is distinguished not by the fact that he or she never suffers a loss, but that on the whole and over time, the

losses are overshadowed by the gains. Derivatives simply provide the mechanism by which these time-honored causes result
in losses today, and to the extent they are misunderstood, the
risk of these losses increases.

Some of the problems with derivatives may not be caused by
imprudent use of these modern tools themselves, but by using
them within a legal and regulatory framework that has not yet
adapted to them. Other problems are the result of the trial-and-
error process, as business and financial managers become more
familiar with these new, complex, and rapidly growing products
which now exist in such huge amounts.

There is no evidence that derivatives are too complex for users
and dealers to evaluate and manage. In fact, the limited incidence
of problems to date provides some preliminary evidence that
many dealers and users succeed in managing their exposure in
appropriate ways and have adapted their corporate decision making to deal with derivatives. The suggestion that derivatives are
contributing to greater systemic risk—or risk to the financial system as a whole—is difficult to evaluate. These are new products,
however, and the best protection from disaster is greater study
and education by those who use them, so that good management
practices will prevail. Every encouragement should also be given
to efforts currently under way to reinforce the legal framework of
their use, particularly in an international context, and to improve
accounting and disclosure requirements.

EXTENT OF USE

According to a recent survey, over 80 percent of private companies consider derivatives either very important or imperative for
controlling risk; 83 percent of financial institutions answered the
same way. Government entities and institutional investors (such
as pension funds) were not included in this survey, but their use
is no less pervasive. The largest uses are for managing existing
and future debt (such as purchasing a cap on a new issue of floating rate debt or swapping one kind of debt for another), managing foreign exchange exposures (swapping an uncertain future
exchange rate for a fixed one), and controlling commodity price
risks.

How much money is invested in derivatives? As we discussed in chapter 1, a common measure of activity is the notional amount of the investment. For example, an investor in cattle futures can purchase one cattle contract—40,000 pounds of cattle—with a margin deposit of only $1,200. If cattle are currently worth 40¢ a pound, 40,000 pounds of cattle are worth $16,000, so the investor can enter a contract requiring him or her to purchase or sell $16,000 of cattle with a margin deposit of only $1,200, or 7.5 percent; $16,000 is the notional amount of the contract. In an interest rate swap, the notional amount of the contract is the amount on which the interest rate payments are based.

The notional value of interest rate and currency swaps outstanding was $3,872 billion at the end of 1991—almost $4 trillion. Of these, about $2 trillion were entered in 1991—double the amount entered in 1989 and four times the amount entered in 1987. This type of derivative use is clearly growing, but the total size is still small compared to other markets. For comparison, the total notional principal of all contracts in the publicly traded futures and options markets was $140 *trillion;* that of bonds $14.4 trillion; that of stocks and equities $10.1 trillion. Currencies trade $1 trillion a day. The gross domestic product of the United States is under $6 trillion.

According to the senior deputy comptroller for capital markets, the fourth quarter 1994 figures for U.S. commercial banks showed that their total holdings in derivatives had increased from roughly $5 trillion in 1990 to slightly over $15 trillion by the end of 1994. The top 25 commercial banks accounted for roughly 97 percent of that activity, with 608 commercial banks accounting for the remaining 3 percent.

MEASURING RISK

The notional value measurement gives very little information about the risk each user of these derivatives has undertaken. For example, a one-year swap might have the same notional value as a ten-year swap, but it is clear the ten-year swap is much riskier since it has a much greater exposure to large interest rate changes. Also, this measurement gives no indication whether the derivative is being used as a hedge, as a proxy for an underlying investment, or for speculation. If it is a hedge, the user's net risk may be reduced to near zero. If it is a proxy, the user's risk is the same as that of the underlying investment. If it is speculative, the risk can obviously vary immensely, increasing in proportion to the amount of leverage used, which in turn depends on the amount of cash the user has deposited as margin or set aside to back the trade.

The risk of a derivative can be very specialized. For example, a CMO floater tranche increases in value as interest rates fall; if it is a superfloater, it will increase by a multiple of the underlying interest rate. A complex, financially engineered debt issue or swap may have payments based on a variety of different indexes and include embedded options. Assessing these risks can be intricate, even though, in principle, derivatives share the same risks as other investments, including market risk, leverage, credit risk, operational risk, and legal risk.

Market Risk

Market risk is what most people first think of as investment risk: the extent to which the value of the investment may decline depending upon market conditions or the success of the underlying business or asset. The extent to which market value fluctuates is called *volatility*, which is measured statistically as the standard deviation of price changes over a period of time. The notional value figure tells nothing about market risk.

Statistical measures of market risk, such as standard deviation, allow an investor to determine, with various degrees of confidence, the probability of loss of specified percentages of the investment at any given time. Price history also allow the prediction of ranges of probable rates of return on the investment over a period of time. However, as stated in every investment disclosure, past performance is no guarantee of future results. The statistical projections are based on the assumption that the future will be like the past, and that underlying market conditions will not change. This has not proven to be a safe assumption in predicting future rates of return.

Use of leverage multiplies the market risk; 5-to-1 leverage will multiply the percentage gains and losses of an investment by 5 (adjusted slightly for the cost of the leverage).

Many derivatives involve greater market risks than other investments, or than the underlying assets on which they are based, because they are leveraged. Others may create market risk that is simply harder to calculate. For example, a CMO tranche will still be subject to prepayment risk, just like the underlying mortgage, but the different tranches will be subject to this risk to different degrees. Some may reduce exposure to the risk, while others will increase it, and perhaps tie in some other factors. More complex derivatives may have cash flows that depend upon a number of different indexes, and also contain more than one embedded option. These are not necessarily riskier than other investments, but modeling their outcomes requires a much higher degree of sophistication. It is more like chess than tic-tac-toe.

Market risk can be limited by the use of derivatives as a hedge. Although a hedged investment is still subject to market risk, and by itself may be extremely risky, the overall portfolio risk may theoretically be reduced to zero in a hedge. However, hedges are often subject to new market risks, such as the possibility that changes in the price of the index used for the hedge will no longer correspond to changes in the price of the underlying investment in the expected way. Another important factor is the timing match between the investment and the hedge. That is, will the cash received from the hedge arrive in time to pay the losses incurred on the hedged investment? As the Metallgesellschaft example in chapter 10 demonstrates, this may not necessarily be the case.

Credit Risk

Credit risk is the risk that the other party to the contract (that is, the counterparty) will fail to perform his or her obligations. If a diner fails to pay a restaurant bill, the restaurant has lost the entire value of the meal. If you are involved in an interest rate swap in which you are receiving a fixed rate in exchange for a variable rate, and the other party defaults, the risk is harder to calculate. It is very unlikely that the whole notional value is at risk—rather, it is the benefit of the swap that is lost. If interest rates have fallen (and the other party would have no other reason to default), you will be unable to replicate the swap at the original cost.

Credit risk is often measured by replacement cost. If the counterparty defaults, perhaps because of insolvency, the investor may immediately find another counterparty and enter the same swap at a higher cost. That replacement cost represents the loss from the failed credit. Replacement costs are almost always a small fraction of the notional principle—usually under 10 percent. For large users, net replacement costs may be even lower, as the profits of some defaulted obligations are netted against the losses of others.

Credit risk is not a serious factor in listed options and futures, in which the exchange itself acts as a counterparty, marking to market the value of every contract at the close of each day's trading and immediately collecting margin deposits in cash to ensure that every participant has more than enough cash on deposit to meet his or her obligations. Swaps and other OTC derivatives face a greater default risk, but they also tend to be limited to counterparties with high credit ratings.

Large private investors, as well as dealers who act as counterparties, also control credit risk in a manner similar to the futures exchanges. On their own books, they can and should mark their investments to market daily, and the contract can require a counterparty who is losing money under the contract to provide adequate security to ensure that those losses will be met.

The contract documents can also call for *netting* during closeouts. Since much of the business in swaps flows through a relatively small number of banks and dealers, the two counterparties to any given transaction may also be counterparties to each other for various other swaps. Under one swap, party A will owe money to party B; under another, B will owe money to A. In some bankruptcy situations, if A goes bankrupt, B may have to pay the money he or she owes A to A's trustee in bankruptcy for division among A's creditors, but B may have to stand in line with all of those other creditors to eventually collect some portion of the money owed to B by A. However, if the contracts between A and B contain a legally enforceable netting provision on A's bankruptcy, B may be able simply to offset the money owed by A against the money B owes to A. In that way, B's loss is limited to A's net obligation to B, not the entire amount that A owes to B.

Netting can significantly reduce the overall effects of credit and settlement risks. The Federal Reserve estimates that netting would reduce the overall credit risk in the swap system, measured by replacement cost, by around 40 percent.

Legal Risk

This is the risk that the derivative contract will not be enforced. Netting agreements, for example, were not honored under U.S. bankruptcy laws until a June 1990 amendment to the U.S. Bankruptcy Code added a provision allowing a U.S. creditor corporation to net its swap exposures with a defaulting counterparty. The Financial Institutions Reform, Recovery, and Enforcement Act (FIRREA) of 1989 gives U.S. commercial banks and thrifts the same ability. The enforceability of netting agreements varies from country to country and in international transactions between counterparties in different countries. Universal recognition of netting agreements would do much to reduce systemic risk in the international financial community.

Even financially capable counterparties can refuse to pay if they successfully defend themselves in court. Derivatives may pose greater legal risk than other investments because of their novelty and complexity. Because they combine the features of traditional contracts, together with those of securities regulated by the SEC and its body of laws, and futures regulated by the CFTC and its body of laws, it is sometimes unclear which set of laws will apply to a given situation. Also because of their novelty, there have been few cases deciding these issues in the courts or before regulatory bodies, and so there is little precedent to guide derivative users and their lawyers. Even the recent spate of lawsuits has not resolved these issues: Because most of these cases are being settled out of court, the body of written judicial and regulatory decisions to guide practitioners is emerging only slowly.

The legal issues in determining who must bear a loss include the question of whether the seller made adequate disclosures to the buyer concerning the product being sold and the question of who was responsible for determining whether a particular investment was suitable for a particular investor's use of it. Some investors claim to have been defrauded. In other cases, investors have claimed that they were never authorized to make the investments in the first place, so the sales should be rescinded. Other investors have claimed that derivative contracts are no different than gambling contracts and therefore are unenforceable.

Legal risk is best avoided by the use of clear, written contracts between the parties to establish who is responsible for determining the suitability of the investment for a particular use, written disclosures by sellers to define the characteristics and risks of an investment, and legal opinions to confirm the buyer's authority to enter the transaction and the enforceability of contractual arrangements.

Operational Risk and the Lack of Transparency

This is the risk of loss caused by inadequate management and oversight structure and controls. An organization runs operational and transparency risks to the extent it does not have in place reliable information systems by which managers can and do calculate and monitor risks and act on a timely basis to control them. A derivative user should be able to accurately identify each of the risks involved in the various derivative contracts that the user has entered and determine the net exposure to these risks on a firmwide basis. This can be a complex undertaking, particularly if many such contracts have been entered. Marking these contracts to market so that the user knows the size of its paper profits or losses on them and of its exposure to counterparty credit may also be a time-consuming and complex task. Unless the user has adequate information systems in place to identify and quantify the risks either internally or through outside providers, the user cannot know the extent of the risks it is running or react on a timely basis to reduce the risks if they threaten to become overwhelming. Within an organization, the temptation to conceal losses by those responsible for those losses must be recognized; measures can be taken so that those who calculate the losses are not the same as those who incur them. Obviously, the greater the market risk, credit risk, or legal risk, the more management attention and oversight is required, and the greater the operational risk should it be lacking.

Systemic Risk

Beyond the risks run by any individual organization, systemic risk refers to the risk exposure of the entire system. Those concerned with derivative risk in this context have pointed to the shear size of the market, its recent rapid growth, the complexity of some derivative instruments, the high leverage that can be employed, and the concentration of activity in a relatively small number of dealers. On a more general level, there is fear that derivatives have tightened the links within the world economy through the widespread use of swaps and other financial instruments based on a variety of international indexes. These concerns have been the subject of hearings, investigations, and studies on a national and international level.

A major study of this subject was conducted by the Group of Thirty, an international body composed of governmental authorities and major private institutions. The study concluded that while efforts to improve risk management within individual institutions must continue, together with legal reforms on national and international levels, the use of derivatives in itself need not substantially increase systemic risk. The study noted that the size of the derivatives market is large, but measures of notional value greatly overstate risk. Also, it found no evidence that most users of derivatives are unable to cope with their complexity.

The study also noted that risk arising from the concentration of derivative activity among a relatively small number of institutions is reduced by the international diversity of these institutions, and the variety of institutions that are involved. Further, this concentration is not necessarily large in relation to other financial activities. Swaps are still predominantly used by larger institutions, which may also explain some of the market concentration. The top eight swap dealers accounted for 58 percent of the interest and currency swaps at the end of 1991, and no firm had more than 10 percent of the market. Overall, there are 150 International Swaps and Derivatives Association (ISDA)-approved swap dealers—three times as many as the number of primary dealers in U.S. government bonds.

Finally, the wave of losses and lawsuits which has recently caused much publicity and concern has been absorbed by the system as a whole without triggering the kind of domino effect that would endanger the system as a whole and cause losses even to those not directly connected to the derivative losses. Furthermore, some research suggests that the increased interconnection of large financial markets does not necessarily increase the volatility of the underlying markets.

SUMMARY OF RISK

As illustrated, derivatives can involve market, credit, legal, and operational risks, but users and dealers can respond to these risks in appropriate ways. Risk is unavoidable in business and in investment; to eliminate risk is to eliminate the opportunity for profit. The use of derivatives on a massive scale is a recent development, however, and as the number of users and types of uses has greatly increased, the understanding of the risks associated with derivatives, and the methods of controlling them, must become widespread as well. Only in this way can individuals and individual institutions limit their risks appropriately. As this is done, and as the law develops so that the legal consequences of derivative use become more predictable in national and international contexts, systemic risk will decline accordingly.

The present popular conception of "risky" derivatives results from a lack of popular understanding of derivatives, particularly in failing to distinguish safe uses of derivatives from risky ones. This in part results from the tendency in press accounts to lump together under one word, *derivatives,* all of the many very different products and uses involved. As we have seen, some add risk, some decrease it by hedging. Derivatives are sometimes characterized as gambling, just as common stocks were so characterized in the past. Both stocks and derivatives involve risks, and indeed derivative investments can involve more risk than stock investments, or less. The difference in risk levels may be directly determined by the amount of leverage employed.

As we have also seen, some uses of derivatives are much more analogous to buying insurance or writing insurance than they are to gambling. (Of course, insurance could also be characterized as gambling. By buying insurance, you are gambling that your house will burn down so that you can collect an insurance settlement in exchange for your premium, and the insurance company is gambling that it won't.) Just as insurance is socially useful to limit individual risks, so are derivatives. Like derivatives, insurance involves a credit risk. If your insurance company fails, you may not collect on your policy. Insurance also involves legal risks relating to the exclusions under an insurance policy document just as complex as many derivative contracts, and which may be subject to court interpretation in the event of a dispute. Operational and transparency risks are encountered if you do not fully understand your insurance policy or if you have not documented the value of your insured property—for example, by photographs, appraisals, and copies of sales receipts available to substantiate a claim in case of the property's loss. Insurance can even involve systemic risk, if the losses of an earthquake or other natural disaster, or even human failures such as the collapse of the savings and loan industry, are too great for the insurance carriers to bear.

Popular fear of derivatives is often based on their complexity and the related fears that either (1) they are not understood by those who use them, so that a global financial meltdown is possible, or (2) that those who sell them understand them all too well, and will use that understanding to take advantage of buyers who don't understand them. Both of these fears can be eliminated by the simple expedient of refusing to buy something you don't understand unless it is well understood by someone you trust. A trusted adviser can help you decide whether your plan for the derivative product fits your purpose, after you define that purpose and the level of risk you are willing to take to achieve it.

10

Derivative Disasters

These case studies illustrate that disasters are usually caused not merely by the use of derivatives, but rather by a combination of traditional factors: excessive use of leverage, inadequate monitoring of traders, and a failure to match the time frames of investments to a company's liquidity requirements. The complexity of derivatives adds to these problems, and suggests that derivatives need closer management scrutiny than other investments, especially when leverage is involved. Nevertheless, it is unlikely that any of these disasters would have come as a complete surprise if they received 1 percent of the attention before the disasters that they did afterward. These cases involve facts now in dispute in civil and criminal litigation so the facts described here are hypothetical. Whatever the ultimate outcome of these disputes, it is clear that they are disasters for many of the people involved, and that some of these disasters were avoidable.

LEVERAGE: WHY WERE THE ORANGE COUNTY LOSSES A SURPRISE?

In finance, as in other fields, those who are unaware of history may be doomed to repeat it, or at least to be very surprised by events that are no more than a variation on similar past events. Almost everyone was surprised at the 20 percent losses in Orange County's investment pool. The truly surprising thing is that anyone was surprised.

Orange County filed for bankruptcy a few days after reporting that its government investment pool had lost $1.5 billion, or 20 percent of the $7.5 billion entrusted to the pool for investment. Newspaper reports in the first few days were full of amazement at the $1.5 billion loss on a portfolio that had produced high returns for several years and was invested in bonds of very high credit quality.

Despite the public reaction, no one familiar with the pool's investment policy, the principles of leverage, and the price behavior of high-quality bonds in the past should have been very surprised.

The pool reportedly had disclosed its investment policy of investing in a portfolio of bonds, and of using leverage to enhance its return. Much has also been written about the complex derivatives used by the pool: inverse floaters, structured notes, and other derivative securities that may have been part of the pool's portfolio. But even without detailed analysis of these investments, knowledge of the type of investment and the effects of leverage alone should have alerted an observer to the possibility of occasional double-digit losses in the pool.

Even the highest-grade bonds have always fluctuated in price, as interest rates rise and fall. The market value of a bond fluctuates because a bond must be held for a number of years before it is paid in full at face value, and during the interim interest is normally paid on the bond at a fixed rate determined when the bond is issued. If this fixed interest rate is higher than prevailing interest rates at any given time, then the bond will sell at a premium. If the fixed rate is lower than other prevailing rates at the time, then the bond will sell at a discount. So a bond can sell at a higher or lower price than its face value even if everyone expects it will be paid in full at its maturity date, simply because during the interim the holder of the bond receives a fixed interest rate that is higher or lower than prevailing interest rates.

If history is any guide, investors in five-year notes could expect gains and losses in the market value of their notes. Of course, if the notes are held to maturity, those gains or losses won't matter: The investor will receive exactly the face amount of the note. But if the notes are sold before maturity, the fluctuations in market value will matter a great deal.

Now add leverage to the analysis. When the Orange County investment pool bought notes, it did not pay cash. It bought more notes than its cash resources permitted by borrowing against its financial assets. (If it bought notes worth several times the amount of cash in the pool, this is just like buying a house with a down payment.)

As we saw with the example of the house purchase, this policy can lead to high rewards, but only at the cost of equally high risk. The underlying investment is the same, and there is exactly the same *pattern* of losses whether or not leverage is used; but the *percentage* profits and losses are multiplied by the amount of leverage used.

Based on the historical record, investors should have been anticipating the possibility of double-digit losses. What is truly amazing is that everyone was surprised when it happened—after all this time that people have been using leverage, its results should not be surprising to even an amateur investor. High leverage is a fine way to turn a pittance into a fortune, and vice versa. It is a powerful tool, which must be used with knowledge and care. The Orange County reaction is particularly surprising in view of the fact that not long before the disaster, these investment policies had been openly criticized in a public election. The incumbent was widely praised for the high returns these investments were earning, and won the election. Unfortunately, he went on to plead guilty to criminal charges, at which time his challenger was appointed to the then-vacant post. Evidently, the electoral process is not a good forum for analysis of investment risks, and voters, like other people, prefer to ignore high risks when they are receiving high returns.

BARING'S PLC: THE TRADER'S OPTION

The Baring's disaster is a textbook example not only of the risks of leverage, but of the need to adequately monitor traders who make huge leveraged investments. Nick Leeson was in charge of exploiting arbitrage opportunities on the Nikkei 225 futures contract. The Nikkei 225 is an index future similar to the S&P 500 index future. The arbitrage opportunities arose from the fact this futures contract was traded on two different exchanges, the Osaka Securities Exchange (OSE) in Japan and the Singapore International Monetary Exchange (SIMEX) in Singapore, but the price of the contract was not always exactly the same on both exchanges. By using large amounts of capital and computerized trading, Leeson undertook to exploit the small price differences between the two markets. Huge amounts were invested, but the risk was relatively very small. The idea was to offset a long position in the market trading at the lower price with an equal short position in the market trading at the higher price, so that the profit would come as the price differential disappeared, and any increase in the price level of the Nikkei 225 that was reflected in both markets (as any large move would be) would have no effect on the value of the position.

However, Leeson soon moved beyond this low-risk arbitrage and began to use strategies in which substantial amounts could be made or lost. These ultimately included outright positions on the market, buying leveraged Nikkei futures in one market without selling an offsetting contract in the other market. Another risky trade was an option strategy known as a *straddle*. Under this strategy puts and calls are both sold. This is equivalent to writing an insurance policy against both price increases and price decreases. A premium is collected, but if the stock or index moves up or down outside the band, the speculator's losses are potentially limitless. Leeson was betting that nothing much was going to happen to the price of the stock. Unfortunately, the Kobe earthquake was disastrous not only for the inhabitants of Kobe, but for Leeson, as the Nikkei 225 Index dropped suddenly. Losses were large, but since Leeson was in charge of the reporting function as well as the trading, he was able to conceal them, as he had been doing on a smaller scale for some time in the past.

Leeson never did cut his losses, until he had to flee the country. Instead, he seems to have adopted the strategy known as the *trader's option*. Seeing his chances for another huge year-end bonus go down the drain, Leeson must have felt he had nothing more to lose except his job (which he might have lost anyway), and a lot to gain if he recouped his loss. So instead of cutting his losses he increased the size of his trades, betting that a rise in prices would create more than enough gains to offset his losses. He invested so much money in this strategy that he may even have hoped to influence a price change through his position. But the index continued to fall, and even his last ditch effort to hedge his Nikkei futures by taking an offsetting position in Japanese interest rates and government bonds failed. (There is often a relationship between stock prices and interest rates.) By the end, Barings held $7 billion in Nikkei 225 futures and $20 billion in government bonds and interest rate futures. The losses were over $1 billion, and the bank was unable to meet its margin calls as its positions were liquidated under distress conditions.

Barings apparently never intended to permit Leeson to take large, unhedged positions on the futures index. He was only authorized to take small risks with large amounts of money, but instead he took large risks with large amounts of money. As a rogue trader, he was apparently able to stray far outside the limits of the trading authority his superiors thought they had given him. Internal controls were so lacking that even the future exchange's margin requirements failed to prevent disaster. As Leeson's losses mounted, the Singapore exchange marked his positions to market daily, and began demanding huge amounts of cash. Barings wired $800 million to meet these margin calls in little more than a month.

At first, commentators theorized that Barings management must simply have assumed Leeson would never take such large positions without hedging them. Later reports suggested that Leeson had actually developed an elaborate strategy to disguise what he was doing by filtering it through dummy accounts. But Barings is no less to blame for this failure. Leeson was in the unusual position of having charge not only of trading, but of monitoring the trading; with better checks and balances, his subterfuges would have been much more difficult, if not impossible.

If a trader has the *potential* to expose a company's assets to the point of potential bankruptcy, any prudent manager will monitor that trader's activities very carefully—especially if that trader begins to post huge losses. Failure to do so is hardly the fault of derivatives themselves, or even of misunderstanding the risks involved in their use, but rather of a lack of controls sufficient to timely alert upper management to the fact that a trader is doing something very different from that which was authorized. The failure of this grand old investment bank—established so long ago that it had financed the Louisiana Purchase—illustrates an even older old idea—the need for adequate management controls.

A FAILED HEDGE: METALLGESELLSCHAFT

One of the legendary cases in contract law involves Westinghouse's long-term contracts to supply uranium to its nuclear power generators at a fixed price. Long-term, fixed-price supply contracts are always dangerous, especially when the supplier does not itself own the commodity being supplied, but will have to buy it on the open market. Westinghouse had committed to supply uranium at around $7 a pound to numerous utilities across the country. After the collapse of OPEC, uranium prices began a dramatic rise, eventually reaching over $40 a pound. (Toward the end of the ensuing lawsuits, Westinghouse was actually unable to obtain uranium at any price, lending some credence to their claim that they were the victim of an international uranium cartel intent on destroying Westinghouse's role in supplying cheap uranium.) Westinghouse was forced to default on the contracts, and eventually paid over $900 million to settle the resulting lawsuits for breach of contract.

When the large German metals and mining conglomerate Metallgesellschaft (MG) entered into similar long-term contracts to supply petroleum to its customers, it hedged the risks of an increase in petroleum prices by investing in the petroleum futures market. But petroleum prices actually fell, eventually reaching a three-year low, and in the process MG began to lose large sums under its futures contracts, sums on which it had to make good very promptly as those contracts were marked to market.

At this point, MG was forced to face two problems with the design of its hedge strategy. First, there was a timing mismatch between its long-term petroleum supply contracts and the petroleum futures and forwards it had used to hedge them in the public and private markets. Losses in the futures contracts occurred in the present. The profits that MG hoped to make on its petroleum supply contracts, in contrast, would only accrue over a long period of time, as the petroleum supply contracts were fulfilled. Second, maintaining the hedge became even more expensive. Each futures contract was written to last for only a few months, rather than the many years involved in the supply contracts. As the delivery date approached under each futures contract, it was necessary to sell the contract and buy a new contract with a delivery date further in the future, *rolling over* the contract in order to maintain the hedge. At the outset, contracts for distant delivery were selling at lower prices than contracts for nearby delivery (a condition known as *backwardation*), so that the new hedges could be purchased at prices lower than the old. As market conditions moved from backwardation to *contango*, in which contracts for distant delivery are more expensive than contracts for nearby delivery, the new hedges had to be purchased at prices higher than the old, and maintaining the hedge became significantly more expensive.

MG reached a point where the present losses were so large and notorious that the company decided not to maintain the hedged position. It took its losses on the hedge and extricated itself from its long-term supply contracts, all at great expense.

After the fall, some commentators argued that MG failed to cut its losses soon enough, and others argued that its hedge strategy was actually sound and would have succeeded in the long run had it been maintained, rather than cut too early. In any case, it is clear that top MG management was not prepared for the high short-term cost of the hedge, even if the negative cash flow could be more than recouped in later years under the long-term supply contracts. MG had adequate resources to finance the wait, but did not expect the financing of this hedge strategy to become such an important part of its overall business.

However, there may have been additional motives for using the strategy adopted, as there were safer alternatives for a pure hedge. MG may have deliberately entered into an imperfect hedge based on an expectation that petroleum prices would not fall as far as they did. As one alternative hedging strategy, MG could have contracted with one of the large derivatives dealers for a long-term custom-made hedge against the market risk of oil prices. For its part, the derivative dealer would have then limited its own risk on the contract either by entering short-term futures contracts (with financing in place to carry adverse short-term price movements) or perhaps by entering into a long-term contract to purchase oil from a company with large oil reserves who wanted to be sure of selling oil at a fixed price in the future. This would have been much like the currency forward contracts discussed earlier, in which the timing of the obligation would have been matched with the timing of the hedge.

Quite apart from the way in which derivatives affect the underlying business decision to enter into this hedge, the underlying long-term, fixed-price petroleum supply contract was itself extremely risky. This was the type of risk that had threatened to bankrupt Westinghouse, and which could have been avoided by entering long-term contracts to obtain the needed oil from an oil company, either directly or through the mechanisms offered in the derivative markets. The decision to take the risk of long-term supply contracts could have been hedged by assuring a source of supply. Instead, a decision was made to employ a very imperfect hedge, matching long-term supply contracts with short-term hedges, leading to negative short-term cash flows, which surprised top management and led to abandonment of the strategy. Evidently, even this well-run company did not have mechanisms in place sufficient to alert top management to the risks that were being run—before they became embarrassingly obvious.

BANKERS TRUST

Bankers Trust made an early and successful bet on derivatives—it bet they would become so important that it made dealing in them a very important part of its business. The company soon became famous not only as a specialist in derivatives, but for designing extremely complex derivatives. In 1993, however, it became the target of several lawsuits based on some of those same products.

The first involved a swap entered into by Gibson Greetings, involving the infamous "LIBOR-squared swap," whereby Gibson swapped a fixed rate of interest for a floating rate that depended partially on the square of a LIBOR index rate. Gibson soon lost about $23 million on the deal. Gibson claimed that Bankers Trust had misrepresented the facts in selling the swaps, and also that Bankers Trust had a fiduciary obligation to Gibson Greetings and failed to adequately advise Gibson as to whether the investment was suitable for them. Later, Procter & Gamble sued Bankers Trust on similar grounds.

These suits raised the question of whether derivatives are so complicated that even a large investor such as P&G is unable to adequately assess their risk. Undeniably, derivatives based on exponential index values, or even multiple indexes, are complex. But it does not take much more than high school math to realize that a variable rate based on the square of an index is extremely volatile. The P&G and Gibson Greetings personnel must have known that substantial risks were potentially involved. (See figure 10.1.)

However, they may not have tracked these values within their own organizations, using information sources and computer models independent of the Bankers Trust personnel with whom they were dealing. Indeed, one accusation in the lawsuit was that the Bankers Trust personnel were able to understate the amount Gibson was losing on the deals.

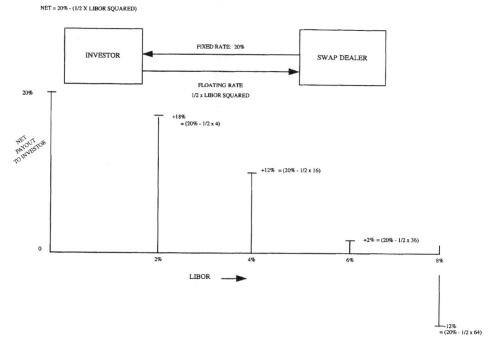

Figure 10.1 LIBOR squared swap.

Large companies are able to value and model complex derivatives independently. The issue is whether they are obliged to do so, or whether they may rely on personnel in the counterparties who have sold them the derivatives, in this case at Bankers Trust, to provide this information. The central allegation seems to be that the sales reps on whom they relied for information took advantage of the situation to sell them products that were simply not very good—they had very little potential for gain and exposed Gibson and P&G to huge losses. Because of these aggressive sales tactics, possible misrepresentation, and perhaps a certain amount of gullibility on the part of Gibson and P&G, they bought products with risks greater than they now admit they knew.

This litigation has less to do with derivatives than with unscrupulous salespeople. Of course, the complexity of the derivative instruments may have made misunderstanding the risks easier, innocently or otherwise. And once again, the addition of leverage (or squared indexes) increased the risks. But lacking misrepresentation, there is no reason to assume that large investors are unable to understand the risks of trades they are involved in. Nobody makes corporate investors buy anything. As another client noted after the Bankers Trust litigation: "We reject nine out of every ten ideas that are brought to us. . . . If I have a difficult time understanding the trade, we will probably tend to back off." This is sound advice.

CONCLUSION

These examples demonstrate that a recent spate of disasters involves derivatives, and that users of derivatives must understand them. But in each case the cause of the disaster was not the derivatives, but misuse of them for the kinds of human reasons that have caused many other disasters. There is little indication that derivatives alone are responsible for increasing systemic risk. Of course, derivatives are complicated, but the wealth of opportunities they provide for greater risk management and financial innovation makes them worth the extra effort to understand and to use properly. No regulatory solution can be designed that will leave us with only the benefits of derivatives and none of the risks, but these risks can be hedged in a very traditional way: Better management systems and controls, along with audits to help confirm that such management systems are in place. In addition, the overall state of affairs may be improved through more stringent disclosure requirements and accounting standards. These are discussed in more depth in chapter 11.

11

Derivative Regulation

Because the extensive use of derivatives is a modern phenomenon and because, by their nature, derivatives implicate elements of many other financial products, the question of regulation
of derivatives, by whom and in what way, is often discussed. In
the wake of some of the recent disasters, it has become a very
politically charged question. The frequency with which derivatives cross national borders, sometimes to circumvent regulatory
restraints in national capital markets, and the fact that they are
causing an ever greater interdependence among the world's capital markets, has not escaped the observation of international
regulatory bodies. In this chapter, we will outline the basic regulatory structure in the United States, and we'll mention some of
the industry trade groups that have been actively working for
improvements in the system. Many of the proposals for improvement have centered on issues of internal controls, adequate
disclosure, and a clear delineation of responsibilities among
counterparties. These issues will be discussed in more detail in
chapter 12.

OPTIONS AND FUTURES

Brokers in futures and options on futures are futures commission merchants (FCM) regulated by the Commodities Futures Trading Commission (CFTC). Brokers in stock and stock index options are regulated by the Securities and Exchange Commission (SEC). Both are also subject to the requirements of the individual exchanges on which each contract is traded. Futures may not be traded outside the exchanges; stock options may, but options on securities remain regulated by the SEC even if they are privately negotiated. Only broker-dealers registered with the SEC may deal in options on securities. The regulatory schemes include minimum capital requirements, various disclosure standards, and margin requirements.

OVER-THE-COUNTER (OTC) DERIVATIVES

OTC dealers include affiliates of large banks, securities firms, insurance firms, and other private dealers. So long as they are not dealing with futures or securities these affiliates need not register with the CFTC or SEC. The question of whether a particular contract is a future, a security, or neither, is therefore critical in determining the regulatory regime under which it falls. Today, most privately arranged contracts among commercial parties, such as many swaps and currency forwards, are considered to be neither futures nor securities, though there are some uncertainties in this area, particularly where embedded options are involved.

The largest share of the swap market is held by banks and their affiliates. In a 1991 survey, 19 of the top 24 interest rate and currency swap dealers were banks, four were affiliates of securities firms, and two were affiliates of insurance companies.

The regulation of these dealers depends on both the type of derivative and the nature of the institution. For example, banks that create private derivative contracts in foreign currencies and interest rates are regulated by neither the SEC nor the CFTC, but instead by the Comptroller of the Currency and, in some cases, by the Federal Reserve Board or by state banking regulators.

Banks and bank affiliates are regulated by the various bank regulators no matter what they sell, derivatives or otherwise. Bank affiliates and broker companies are therefore probably the most heavily regulated of OTC dealers, and must comply with capital requirements, limits on leverage, and various disclosure and anti-fraud requirements. The Federal Reserve also has its own set of regulations affecting banks and broker-dealers, and state "blue-sky" laws may apply as well.

Securities firms and FCM are regulated by the SEC and CFTC. In the wake of some of the recent derivative-related disasters, these disclosure requirements may increase. In fact, some of the largest securities firms have already voluntarily agreed to provide more detailed information to the regulators—but not necessarily to the public at large or to their shareholders.

Insurance firm affiliates and insurance firms in general are subject to no federal regulation. They are regulated by state insurance commissioners, but most states do not have examination or capital requirements for derivative affiliates, and the reporting requirements usually do not include separate detail on derivatives but are limited to consolidated financial statements from the parent firm. State insurance regulations, however, also include stringent limitations on the types of investments and investment strategies which may be used.

The boundary lines between these agencies are not always clear. The particular terms of a derivative contract may determine whether its issuance is subject to the jurisdiction of the SEC, the CFTC, or neither. Even expert attorneys may come to differing conclusions in the case of particular contracts. In addition, the fiduciary and disclosure requirements that apply to the sale of a particular derivative product may depend upon the regulatory regime under which it falls. For example, the recent Bankers Trust litigation included charges based on both SEC and CFTC disclosure requirements.

QUASI REGULATION: TRADE GROUPS, ACCOUNTING STANDARDS, AND RATING AGENCIES

Each regulated industry has its own trade association, which often serves as an intermediary between a particular company and the regulators. Self-regulation of the futures industry is carried out by the National Futures Association, a private body under the supervision of the CFTC. Similarly, self-regulation of securities brokers and dealers is carried out by the National Association of Securities Dealers (NASD) and by the New York and other stock exchanges under the supervision of the Securities and Exchange Commission.

Many accounting questions arise in the classification of derivatives, which are resolved by accounting firms under guidelines established by the Federal Accounting Standards Board (FASB), an accounting industry association. For example, when a company enters a swap, it acquires both an obligation to make future payments and a right to receive future payments. Hence a swap is an *executory contract* (a contract in which both parties have future performance obligations), so the notional principal amount of the swaps are not recorded on the balance sheets. The FASB has been particularly challenged by the rapid growth of the derivative business and the many accounting issues that require resolution. Standards to resolve these issues are reviewed in appropriate cases by the SEC, CFTC, and other governmental regulatory bodies. Financial statements must incorporate any disclosures mandated by the accounting rules, and these disclosures are in the process of development and evolution.

One of the most challenging and pivotal roles in the derivatives business falls to the private rating agencies such as Moody's and Standard & Poor's, whose credit ratings grade the derivatives issued by any particular organization. Indeed, many banks and brokerage houses have established very well capitalized subsidiaries to conduct their derivatives business in order to obtain the highest possible credit rating for those derivatives. Examples of these AAA-rated subsidiaries include Morgan Stanley Derivatives Products, Goldman Sachs Financial Products, Salomon Brothers Special Purpose Derivative Vehicles, and Paribas Special Purpose Derivative Vehicles. The higher the credit rating, the more salable the derivative products that the organization issues. Determination of the credit rating requires careful examination of the organization's financial statements and an evaluation of all the risks that the organization runs. This is of course an indispensable function in protecting the integrity of the entire financial system. It is carried out by private rating agencies with a long history of experience in evaluating credit matters, who are applying their expertise to the nuances of this rapidly expanding financial area.

INTERNATIONAL REGULATION

On an international level, these organizations have counterparts in every country. Most of the G7 regulatory bodies are actively examining the derivatives marketplace. Laws, standards, and practices vary from country to country, and their complete description is well beyond the scope of this book.

There are also multinational bodies such as the Group of Thirty and the Bank of International Settlements, whose perspective transcends that of any one nation. The Bank for International Settlements has studied derivatives practices and proposed specific recommendations for their improvement. The Group of Thirty is another prestigious international body which has conducted and published a very thorough study on the uses of derivatives, including an analysis of the varying laws and practices from country to country, in a series of volumes that constitute one of the most authoritative works in the area.

12

Controlling Risk

REGULATORY SAFEGUARDS

Safeguards against failure of the world's financial system revolve around an attempt to ensure that individual organizations do not make commitments beyond their ability to fulfill them, or if one does, to ensure that its failure does not trigger a domino effect causing the failure of many other organizations. Of course, it is in no one's interest for this to happen.

No bank or derivatives dealer sets out to take on so much derivative business that a change in market conditions would cause its bankruptcy. Nevertheless, this can happen. The Baring's collapse is an example. Due to the overcommitment of one trader to a risky strategy which was apparently unauthorized by Baring's, this old, large, respected investment banking house suddenly developed more debts than it could pay.

Baring's was an English merchant bank brought down by trading in Singapore and Japan on Japanese stock index futures. No single regulator oversaw all its affairs. The result of this merchant banking failure was that the owners lost all of their investment in it (it was taken over by a Dutch firm which assumed all of its obligations) but none of the customers, or anyone else who did business with Baring's, lost their money. Nor did the failure of Baring's cause any other bank or brokerage house to fail.

In the wake of the Baring's failure and a series of international and domestic troubles involving the derivatives markets, many trade organizations, industry groups, futures and securities regulators, and international bodies are working on the evolving set of safeguards to protect against systemic failure.

Despite the diversity of interests, all of these regulatory and self-regulatory efforts have made three similar suggestions with regard to controlling systemic risk. First of all, organizations involved in derivatives must have sufficient management controls so that they know which risks they intend to take, and they must monitor their activities sufficiently to know which risks they are actually taking. Second, these risks should be published or disclosed in such a way that outside parties dealing with the organization can themselves assess the risk and compare them to the risks of other organizations, rating agencies can grade the risk in relation to the organization's capital, and regulators can review the whole process and take any additional steps they feel are necessary. Third, relationships among parties to derivative transactions must involve a clear understanding of organizational credit risks, the risks of particular transactions, and the respective responsibilities of the parties in evaluating those risks and their appropriateness to the portfolios involved. All of this should be appropriately reflected in general disclosure documents and in agreements regarding particular transactions.

In short, the unifying theme is that users of derivatives need access to accurate information about their investments, and they need better controls to ensure this information is properly used.

DISCLOSURE

Disclosure is a very powerful tool, since it provides people with the information needed to protect themselves. If a bank discloses that it has a much higher exposure to derivatives risks than other banks, people will be reluctant to deal with the riskier bank, lest it become unable to meet its obligations to them. The rating agencies will downgrade the credit rating of the bank, the bank will be worth less to its owners, and the owners will have every incentive to rectify the situation. Competition and self-interest will reward the banks that do not take excessive risks.

One overriding problem with disclosure is that there is not yet universal agreement on how best to measure and express the risk that must be disclosed so that the various derivative dealers can be compared by the same measure. Until standards are agreed upon, however, good internal controls and methods of monitoring risk appropriate to the particular user are all the more important.

INTERNAL CONTROLS

Of course, no individual can ensure that the entire system will not fail. However, if individuals do their best to protect themselves and their beneficiaries in these areas, they will also contribute to protecting the system as a whole.

The Derivatives Policy

As we have seen in our discussion of the legal risks surrounding derivatives, when things go wrong they send repercussions to the very top of the organization. The best protection against things going wrong is for those at the very top to be sure that there is in place within the organization a statement of policy concerning derivatives. Protocols should set out the circumstances in which derivatives can be used, define the limits of the risks to be taken, and empower personnel with responsibility to implement these decisions. These policies cannot be established once and then forgotten. To be effective, policies must be dynamic and constantly reevaluated. In addition, a structure for monitoring compliance with the policy on a frequent basis provides the organization with additional protection. This can include frequent independent checks on the actual contents of the derivatives portfolio, the current market value of the contents of the derivatives portfolio, and the potential risks inherent in that portfolio.

Auditing Portfolio Contents

Independent reports on the actual contents of the derivative portfolio can ordinarily be obtained from the custodian of those assets.
It is important that these custodians have sufficient assets (often
indicated by a high credit rating) so that in the rare event that an
asset is lost or money evaporates due to an inaccurate report, the
custodian will be able to make good the loss.

If the asset is a security, custody is usually held by a bank or
brokerage house, which may actually hold physical custody of the
stock certificate or bond, or in whose name the stock or bond is
being held, sometimes as an electronic entry. Futures contracts are
not represented by physical certificates, but rather by electronic
entries in an exchange clearinghouse. Margin deposits paid by the
customer to the futures commission merchant may be held in the
form of securities deposited by the customer, treasury bills purchased with cash, or cash deposited by the customer that is aggre-
gated with cash deposited by other customers in a segregated
customers account. This money may then be invested in bank
deposits or short-term liquid fixed-income securities as permitted
by the rules of the exchange.

Whether there is a bank, broker-dealer, or futures commission
merchant with custody of the securities or futures contracts,
reports on the content of the portfolio can readily be obtained. In
the case of over-the-counter derivatives custom-made for a particular user, there is ordinarily no security to be placed in the hands
of an independent broker-dealer or custodian, nor is there a
futures contract to be held through an exchange-clearing futures
commission merchant. Instead, there is simply a contractual
agreement between the organization purchasing the derivative
and the counterparty that issued it, which in most cases will be an
affiliate of a bank, broker, or other derivatives dealer.

For an organization with a considerable number of derivatives, it may be necessary to collect reports from the following:
(1) banks and brokers on securities they hold, (2) futures commission merchants on futures contracts they hold, and (3)
sources internal to the organization on derivatives contracts
they have entered into directly with counterparties. In the latter
situation, it may even be useful to confirm this information with
the counterparties themselves. All of this information, gathered

together, is necessary to provide the organization with a view of its current derivatives portfolio.

Marking to Market

In analyzing the content of the portfolio, it is of course important to determine the actual present market value of each element of the portfolio. The value of marketable securities, and the obligations arising from short positions in those securities, can easily be determined by published quotations of prices for those securities in the newspapers and by electronic means. Similarly, the value of futures contracts can easily be determined from the report of the futures commission merchant through which they are held. Indeed, the FCM will credit or debit cash from the customer's account daily to reflect any changes in those values. Like margin calls on securities and short sales, this marking to market and daily cash settlement requirement provides an invaluable reality check on the value of a derivatives portfolio. It forces the user to come to grips with the reality of losses.

In the case of over-the-counter derivatives, which may be custom-made for a particular user rather than traded on an exchange, there is no clearinghouse function that automatically forces recognition of losses in market value. In some cases, it may even be difficult to actually mark them to market, and they may instead be marked to "model." Conceivably, a trader within an organization could conceal these losses out of fear of consequences upon their discovery, until they became so large that they threaten the organization's existence. It may therefore be very helpful to have an independent check within the organization, by a party not reporting to the trader involved, on the market value of all over-the-counter derivatives.

Estimating the Risk of Loss

In addition to independently verifying the actual contents of the portfolio and its value and liabilities today, a complete analysis of an organization's derivative portfolio requires an estimation of the potential gains and losses that may result from holding the portfolio, the probability that risks will become realized losses, and a plan for dealing with this situation if it should begin to occur. A good algorithm should incorporate interest rate risk, equity price risk, bond investment risk, derivatives risk, counterparty risk, currency risk, country risk, liquidity risk, settlement risk, and operational risk. For an extensive derivatives portfolio, this may not be a simple matter—it involves issues of judgment as well as objective measurement—but it is the heart of any risk-control system.

Estimating the risk of loss does involve certain objective elements. For example, when an options contract has been purchased, no more than the purchase price for the option contract can be lost. Similarly, a custom-made derivatives product can include features that limit losses to preestablished amounts. However, in other types of agreements, or in the case of a futures contract or sale of an options contract, there is no mathematical limit to a potential loss. Instead, organizations rely on estimates of the most that could be lost based upon past pricing history and an evaluation of present market conditions. A common risk measurement is a statistical projection of the maximum amount it is probable to lose over a given time period, measured with a 95 percent confidence level. Of course, even this estimate will be wrong 5 percent of the time. It is also possible that market conditions will change so that the statistical basis for the projection is no longer valid. For these reasons, it is also important to simulate worst-case scenarios, such as a sharp rise in interest rates, foreign exchange rates falling outside an established band, and even a stock market crash.

Derivatives dealers invest substantial sums in software and other systems to develop these estimates and apply them to their portfolios. One set of calculations of *value at risk* (VAR) is made available daily on the Internet. It involves calculations of price movements, with those over the last few weeks being weighted most heavily, and provides a figure allowing investors to estimate with various levels of confidence, the maximum amount that could be lost in a day. Using this data, an organization can multiply each asset in its derivative portfolio by the probable loss figure to derive a figure of the total probable loss that the organization could suffer that day.

This is one of many means of calculating the risk run by a derivatives portfolio. It emphasizes very recent price history, so that if price swings become wider, the value at risk may suddenly increase in very substantial amounts. If this happens, the organization must be in a position to reduce its derivative exposure to limits acceptable for the organization.

Exit Plans

Adopting a plan to stop losses once they begin to occur, before they can grow large enough to exceed the comfortable limits of an organization, is a critical part of any risk-control system. As losses mount, there is a natural human tendency to try to pretend it isn't happening. It is very unpleasant to convert paper losses into real losses by exiting the position. The decision to exit forfeits the hope that the market will change direction, proving the original strategy right after all. Refusing to exit maintains the hope that the paper losses will vanish and profits will be made as originally anticipated. It is this blend of denial of losses and hope for vindication that has led many traders to exercise the trader's option discussed earlier and to conceal losses until they become overwhelming.

Protection against exactly this sort of risk can be achieved by a well-defined and well-monitored policy of cutting losses when they reach preset limits. There is nothing novel about such a policy, which amounts to no more than the old investors' maxim of cutting your losses and letting your profits run. Its implementation, however, is never easy in the heat of the moment. For this reason, a well-conceived and well-implemented plan can be critical to protecting an organization from seriously damaging losses.

Even if such a plan exists and the will to implement it remains in the face of unpleasant market trends, its effectiveness can be hampered by extreme price changes in the market and by a disappearance of liquidity. An example of extreme price action occurred in October 1987 in the United States stock market, which lost one-third of its market value in a matter of days. Investors who tried to limit their losses by selling stocks found that they could do so only at prices that may have been well below those at which they had hoped to exit in a worst case. An example of a loss of liquidity occurred in 1994, when the market for collateralized mortgage derivatives shrank to a small portion of its former size. There were many sellers, but few buyers. While events such as this occur only rarely, they may be impossible to predict and they can be devastating, particularly in a highly leveraged portfolio where the losses can far outstrip the assets an organization wishes to commit to the particular position.

Worst Cases: Buying Insurance

Analysis of the possibility of these events can be made through worst-case-scenario modeling, which utilizes not only recent price history, but considers the worst price movements ever to take place in a particular market—or even more extreme price movements. The market for derivatives is large enough so that insurance can be purchased against such eventualities in the form of put options, for example. The price of this insurance is affected by the amount of the "deductible" before it comes into play; that is, the difference between the current market price and the strike price of the option. The bigger the deductible, the less expensive the insurance. Deciding whether to purchase such insurance involves weighing the size of the position to be taken, the effect of possible large losses, the statistical remoteness of that possibility, and the cost of the insurance itself for a given period of time.

The costs of staffing and carrying out this risk-control exercise within an organization, as well as the costs of implementing it by means of purchasing derivatives for risk-control purposes, can be substantial, but neglecting the effort can have very serious consequences. It should be regarded as a way of increasing the net long-term returns from the entire area of activity by reducing the periodic losses that may be suffered in the pursuit of those returns. If the risk-control function is not separated from the trading function, the objectives of the whole organization can be put at risk.

UNAUTHORIZED TRADING

Of course, internal controls can be ignored or purposely circumvented. Major losses have resulted when managers go beyond the bounds of their authority in their trading activities. Safeguards against traders deliberately running unauthorized risks can be very valuable. It may be surprising that this is a frequent cause of loss, but it is. It is a simple matter of people doing what they have been instructed not to do and what they have agreed not to do.

The reasons for this kind of behavior are unclear, but it is clear that it occurs.

When it comes to stockbrokers, for example, one of the most frequent grounds of customer complaints leading to arbitration is that of unauthorized trading. Of course, many stockbrokers would never engage in such conduct, and faithfully carry out their customers' instructions. If they cannot persuade the customer to make a trade, than the trade is not made. Sometimes, however, some stockbrokers apparently skip the necessary step of persuading the customer to make the trade. This clear breach of fiduciary duty by an agent acting without the principal's authority is particularly surprising because it is almost certain to be detected. However, some stockbrokers apparently cannot resist the temptation to seize control of the trading themselves, rather than leaving the decision to their customer and restricting themselves to the role of giving advice and carrying out the customer's decision.

This sort of misconduct also takes place on occasion among investment managers. Again, it may occur rarely, but when it does it can have disastrous results. This is particularly true of derivative trading, where high leverage can lead to losses far beyond the funds placed under the investment manager's control. Checks and balances that lead to early detection of any unauthorized trading are very worthwhile.

Examples

Examples of the problems caused by unauthorized trading are all too easy to find, though all are hypothetical since the facts are subject to litigation and dispute.

We have already discussed the case of Nick Leeson, the Barings trader whose apparently unauthorized switch from very safe arbitrage trading to very risky outright positions pushed this centuries-old firm into bankruptcy within a very short space of time. A similar example of apparently unauthorized trading is the Kidder Peabody trader who amassed government bond positions beyond his authority. They remained undiscovered for well over a year as their losses grew in size until the parent corporation, General Electric, was forced to transfer hundreds of millions of dollars to cover the losses. The sale of Kidder Peabody by General Electric followed.

Like General Electric, Procter & Gamble also has a reputation for good management. Nevertheless, P&G also lost over $100 million in derivative trades that according to some accounts were specifically prohibited by Procter & Gamble policy.

An investment partnership run by David Askin attracted some of the country's most sophisticated institutional investors. The partnership was recommended by consultants upon whom pension funds rely, and was supposed to be "market neutral." It would take short positions to balance its long positions, with the intention of reducing the risk and volatility of the derivative portfolio. But trading results nevertheless began to deteriorate, and the general partner was charged with misleading his limited partners about the investment positions and the extent of their losses. The losses mounted, and the partnership foundered in bankruptcy.

The Wisconsin State Investment Board lost over $100 million as the result of unauthorized trades by an investment manager, and the treasurer of Orange County, California, pleaded guilty to criminal charges of unauthorized transfers of assets among investor accounts.

In none of these cases were the individuals involved embezzling or otherwise applying the money that had been entrusted to them for their own benefit. Apparently, they simply thought that they could produce better results for their employers or partners if they traded in unauthorized ways—and earn bigger bonuses for themselves in the process. Perhaps they thought they were smarter than those who had given them their instructions. When the trading went against them, they concealed the mounting losses or even increased the size of their debts, leading to results that were disastrous to them, to their partners or employers, and to their individual supervisors.

One final example concerns the Common Fund, which oversees about $20 billion in endowment money from over 1,400 colleges and universities. When officials of the Common Fund read of some of the misadventures just described, they decided to make sure their own investment managers were following the investment guidelines as instructed. When they began to scrutinize the trading of one of their investment managers who was handling about $1 billion of the Common Fund assets, this well-respected trader confessed that he had not been following the instructions he had been given and that he had incurred over $100 million in losses as a result. The losses had apparently been building for more than two years, and had gone undetected not only by the Common Fund, but by the four partners at the investment management firm where the trader worked.

The trader was supposed to be seeking small arbitrage profits from discrepancies between the prices of individual stocks and of stock indices composed of a basket of such stocks. This trading was to be fully hedged by being long the stocks and short the indices, or vice versa. According to this account from the *Wall Street Journal:* "Three years ago [the trader] did a transaction he wasn't able to hedge before the market closed. He took a small loss, we understand in the low five figures. At that point, he crossed the Rubicon. He was determined not to let the market beat him and tried to get it back. He did a number of things for the next three years that turned what was supposed to be a conservative portfolio into a speculative one, which wasn't authorized." The trader had been with the investment management firm for 12 years and was well regarded in his firm and on Wall Street.

Unauthorized trading can occur anywhere. It can occur in banks or investment banking houses, such as Baring's or Kidder Peabody. It can occur in large, well-run public companies, such as Procter & Gamble or General Electric. It can occur among traders for pension funds, such as Wisconsin, or educational institutions, such as the Common Fund, or in private partnerships. It may not occur often, but when it does the results can be serious.

Detection of Unauthorized Trading

Detection of unauthorized trading seems relatively easy in the case of exchange-traded derivatives, where the futures commission merchant prepares a daily report on activity. This was true in the case of Baring's, except that apparently no one was reading these daily reports except personnel who were reporting to the individual doing the unauthorized trading. Also, detection of unauthorized trading would have required comparison of reports from two different futures commission merchants, the one doing the trading on the Osaka exchange and the one doing the trading on the Singapore exchange, to be sure that the two sets of trades balanced and offset each other. If there were other markets involved, comparison of those markets would have been required as well. Nevertheless, early detection of the problem would have been possible from the records provided by the futures commission merchants.

When over-the-counter derivatives are used instead of exchange-traded derivatives (as in all the cases mentioned other than Baring's and the Common Fund), detection is more difficult because there is no futures commission merchant with the responsibility to provide daily reports on the results, mark every contract to market on a daily basis, and collect more cash daily to cover any losses. As a result, losses can be concealed for a much longer period of time, unless someone within the organization is given the specific assignment of checking on the trader's position.

The importance of very frequent checks on every trader's position by personnel who are independent of that trader can hardly be overemphasized. If the trader is the only person within the organization who understands what he or she is doing, and the only person monitoring the strategy on a daily basis, then the door is open to the kind of problems described here. By definition, every trader entrusted with sums of money large enough to create these kinds of problems is trusted and well respected within his or her organization. In most cases, the trust is justified, but the rare case in which the trust is abused can lead to serious problems for those senior to the trader, up to and including the company's board of directors. In the case of Baring's, everyone senior to the trader left the firm—including Peter Baring whose name the firm bore.

If the firm has a policy on derivatives that spells out with some specificity what the trader may or may not do, and personnel are assigned to closely monitor the trader's activities to ensure that they fall within those parameters, then problems of this kind should be avoided. Organizational structures and costs may make this appear burdensome in particular cases, but without such precautions there is always the risk of unauthorized trading, which may remain undetected as it grows into a truly serious problem.

Part 4

FIDUCIARY RESPONSIBILITIES OF USING DERIVATIVES

INTRODUCTION

Derivatives, like any investment, entail risk. When they are used with leverage, the risk can be correspondingly large. Of course, some risk is unavoidable and anticipated. When losses are large, however, in percentage terms, in terms of the total amount of money lost, and in terms of the surprise or feigned surprise of losers at the extent of the losses, then those who have lost the money begin casting about to see who must take the blame and whether there is anyone else who will make good those losses. Lawsuits are sure to follow, and if you are part of the decision-making process or chain of command, you may find yourself on the receiving end of this litigation, or at least under close scrutiny. To avoid liability, you will have to demonstrate that you did not breach your fiduciary responsibilities as someone who manages other people's money.

If you are managing other people's money, you have a fiduciary duty to those people. A corporate manager or director has a fiduciary duty to the shareholders of the corporation. A mutual fund manager or director has a fiduciary duty to the investors in the mutual fund. A pension fund manager has a fiduciary duty to those people whose comfortable retirement is in his or her hands. In part 4, we examine the nature of those fiduciary duties in general in order to see how they relate to the handling of derivatives in particular.

13

Your Fiduciary Duty

THE DUTY OF LOYALTY AND EXCEPTIONS

Every action taken by a fiduciary must be for the exclusive benefit of those whose money is being managed, not for the benefit of the fiduciary or any other party. This duty is taken very seriously under the law. In holding defendants liable for breach of this duty, judges often quote an opinion written in 1928 by Judge Cardozo: "Not honesty alone, but the punctilio of honor the most sensitive, is . . . the standard of behavior." This strict standard has been applied in the context of corporate law, pension law, mutual fund law, and the laws applicable to universities and charitable institutions. The Internal Revenue Code, for example, includes a long list of prohibited transactions in which fiduciaries might act to benefit themselves.

Of course, fiduciaries such as corporate managers, trustees, pension and university personnel, and mutual fund managers do obtain some benefit for themselves in addition to the satisfaction of helping those whose money they are managing. Most obviously, fiduciaries are paid for their trouble. But they also may sometimes enter into particular transactions that directly benefit their own interests as well as those of the organizations they are managing. In recognition of this, there are various specific exceptions, and in case of doubt, there are procedures for asking the opinion of tax or pension regulators about particular transactions affecting pension funds, universities, or charitable institutions.

In the corporate setting, the compensation of the corporate manager or any other transaction that might benefit the manager as well as the corporation must be approved by a supervisor who obtains no personal benefit from the transaction and who concludes that it is fair and in the best interest of the corporation. This rule applies even at the highest levels of the corporation. For example, a transaction benefiting the chief executive officer, who may also be a director of the corporation, must be approved by a majority of the board of directors (or a compensation committee of the board of directors), none of whom receives any personal benefit from the proposed transactions.

These rules also apply to transactions involving derivatives. An obvious example of a breach of the duty of loyalty would be a fiduciary who accepts personal favors or kickbacks to enter into a derivative transaction with a particular broker or counterparty. Such an obvious breach of duty would incur not only liability for the amount of the favors or payments accepted by the fiduciary and for any damages suffered by the beneficiaries (shareholders, retirees, investors, etc.), but criminal penalties as well.

More subtle and controversial issues involving the duty of loyalty arise when fiduciaries accept no gifts or favors from a third party, but act in a way intended to increase or preserve their compensation within their own organization, but which they know is not in the organization's best interest. Conduct of this kind is often very difficult to identify, and can involve so much second-guessing and hindsight that liability may be impossible to establish unless the fiduciary has actually admitted that he or she intended to benefit personally at the expense of the organization.

An extreme example of this kind of behavior is the *trader's option.* Imagine a derivatives manager who has made an unwise investment despite the best intentions. The market has moved unfavorably, and the manager knows that reporting the situation accurately to superiors will cause immediate liquidation of the investment, absorption of the losses by the firm, and the manager's own instant dismissal. Therefore, instead of reporting the situation accurately to superiors, the manager conceals it in the hope that the market will turn around so that all of the losses may be recouped and perhaps even become profits. The manager knows that this course of action is contrary to the policies of the organization—that it exposes the organization to the risk of even larger losses which could seriously threaten the financial viability of the organization—but to avoid certain disaster, the manager takes the trader's option and conceals the situation.

The danger of this sort of behavior is always present in an organization. An effective safeguard is to have other people who do not share responsibility for the decisions oversee the trader's activity, so that they can report the situation even if the trader does not. This function is often carried out by internal auditors; but auditors can sample the trader's actions only sporadically, and so will not be continuously aware of every trader's every activity. When derivatives and high leverage are involved in ways that could potentially cause serious damage to an organization, more continuous and comprehensive systems should be considered. Before considering these, however, we will discuss the other major duty owed by fiduciaries.

DUTY OF CARE

The other universal fiduciary responsibility is the duty of care. The requirements of this duty are different when applied to different fiduciaries. Pension funds have the most stringent requirements under the duty of care, embodied in the *prudent-investor rule*. Corporations (as well as many universities, charitable institutions, and mutual funds) are allowed much broader latitude under the business-judgment rule.

Business-Judgment Rule

The business-judgment rule allows corporate decision makers to do what they think is best for the corporation. Courts understand that no business is free from risk, and they are reluctant to substitute their own judgment of which risks to run and how to run them (often formulated with the benefit of hindsight) for that of the active managers of the business. Risks must be run, losses sometimes occur, and those losses may even lead to bankruptcy—all despite the best intentions and efforts of the corporate managers. Under the business-judgment rule, so long as there is a business decision taken in good faith, and without any conflict of interest that might breach the duty of loyalty, courts are unlikely to find a breach of the duty of care.

On the other hand, the duty of disclosure under the securities laws can be quite strictly applied, particularly in the case of securities offerings by public companies. The corporate manager is given wide discretion to decide whether the corporation should run a particular risk, but the existence of those risks must be disclosed to the shareholders whose money is being managed. Once the risks are known, shareholders can choose to buy the stock if they feel the opportunity for gain outweighs the risks involved, or they can sell the stock if they do not wish to run the risks. It is assumed the market will price the shares of the stock to reflect investors' appraisal of the risks and opportunities that have been disclosed or which may be obvious from the general business context.

Is There a Duty to Hedge?

The application of this general legal framework of the business-judgment rule to issues involving derivatives raises many business and legal issues that have not yet been resolved.

For example, in the past, many business risks were unavoidable. Even if management had a desire to hedge against the risks, there was often no easy means to do so. Only in the case of foreign currency exposure, where banks have traditionally offered their clients hedging opportunities in the forward market or where there happened to be a regulated futures contract that precisely fit the corporation's needs, could a corporation hedge its risks.

Now, however, with the emergence of trillions of dollars of custom-made, over-the-counter derivatives, there is scarcely any risk against which a business is unable to hedge. Not only may a business hedge its risks, but it can seek new sources of profit by taking risks in this market, and the use of high leverage may offer it the hope of very significant profits in relation to the amount of assets deployed.

This new ability to hedge almost every risk does not necessarily mean that there is a fiduciary duty to do so. Every hedge has a price, just as an insurance policy does. If the hedge is essentially an option, the cost will be an option premium much like an insurance premium. If the hedge is in the nature of a future contract, the hedge will involve lost profit opportunity as well as whatever commission and slippage may be involved. A corporation that hedged every risk would almost certainly lose money, since the combined costs of the hedging premiums and the loss of profit opportunities would exceed whatever opportunities for profit remained.

But this new ability to hedge almost every risk does bring new responsibilities. The task of corporate management is to fully understand the risks that are being undertaken, those that are being avoided, and the extent of each. Such an understanding is needed to make good business decisions, even if courts are not likely to second-guess those decisions. From a legal standpoint, such an understanding is even more critical in making appropriate disclosures to stockholders so that they will know the nature of the corporation's business—the sort of opportunities it has and the risks it is running.

Brane v. Roth: **Duty to Hedge**

The need for care in decisions and disclosures concerning derivatives was made particularly clear in light of an Indiana court decision (*Brane v. Roth*) holding the directors of a grain cooperative liable for failing to sufficiently hedge their grain inventory against the risk of a decline in grain prices. Prices did decline, and the small hedge that the cooperative had used was insufficient to provide much protection. The court found that the directors had failed to adequately instruct and supervise the manager to whom the hedging operation was entrusted. They were held liable—the business-judgment rule was insufficient to protect them. Presumably the members of the cooperative expected price risks to be fully hedged, with no chance of further gain or loss.

While this decision should not be given undue weight, neither can it be entirely dismissed as an aberration. It involved relatively small amounts in a grain cooperative distant from the financial centers where much larger amounts of derivatives originate, and it also seems to be the only case reported to date that has considered this issue. However, a similar unforgiving attitude toward failure to understand and use derivatives has been reflected in the press and in academia. For example, a Barron's editorial recently argued that companies who don't use derivatives are, on the whole, much riskier than companies who do. It also quoted Wharton Business School Professor Richard Marston, who had constructed a study of derivative use by corporations: "Any firm that has an exposure and doesn't have derivatives is gambling with the firm's money."

While no court is likely to go so far as to find a universal duty to hedge every risk through derivatives, this case provides a clear warning of the need to understand derivatives, consider their use in appropriate instances, and make appropriate disclosures to shareholders about the corporation's policies and practices in this area.

Risk is inevitable in business, and the huge growth of derivatives in recent years has done nothing to change that fact. It has simply given to corporate management a much greater variety of methods to select which risks to take, by hedging against some risks through derivatives and by seeking new opportunities for profits (by taking new risks) through other derivative investments.

The Prudent-Investor Rule

Those responsible for the investment of pension funds are subject to more rigorous standards than other corporate decision makers. In the ordinary course of corporate business, managers have broad latitude to take risks, so long as the material facts concerning the business are disclosed to investors. In the case of pension funds, however, managers are not free to pursue a high-risk strategy: Instead, they must behave as prudent investors.

The law defining the conduct of the prudent investor developed over a period of more than 150 years, in the context of private trusts. Those managing other people's money have always been subject to lawsuits when things go awry, and even the best clients sometimes sue their trustees. In the 1830 case of *Harvard College v. Amory* the court defined this responsibility in a timeless manner: Fiduciaries should observe how people of prudence, discretion, and intelligence manage their own affairs, not in regard to speculation, but in regard to the permanent disposition of their funds, considering the probable income as well as the probable safety of the capital to be invested. This statement is often quoted by courts, and it forms the basis for many state and federal statutes and court decisions.

The requirement that a prudent investor must observe the conduct of others and act accordingly keeps this standard of conduct up to date. The prudent investor looks not to yesterday's textbook but to what is happening today in the financial community, and how people of prudence, discretion, and intelligence are behaving. As financial practice changes, the legal standard changes with it.

Although unchanged in this respect, a version of the prudent-investor rule now applicable to most private pension funds is somewhat more specific. It requires that a fiduciary discharge his or her duties with the care, skill, prudence, and diligence under the circumstances then prevailing that a prudent person acting in like capacity and familiar with such matters would use in the conduct of an enterprise of a like character and with like aims. In other words, the standard of comparison for reasonable behavior is explicitly raised to the level of a knowledgeable person in the same field. A similar requirement is found in a proposed Prudent Investor Act drafted by the American Law Institute (ALI) and recommended to state legislators by the American Bar Association.

This rule also makes two other important changes to the older standard: It allows greater delegation of authority and it measures performance by looking at the results of the portfolio as a whole.

Role of Delegation

Curiously enough, the ability to delegate management functions was prohibited under the early versions of the prudent-investor rule applicable to the law of private trusts. The rationale underlying this rule was that the grantor of the trust was relying on the personal skill of the trustee, and that it was a breach of trust to fail to attend to business oneself and hand the responsibility over to another, no matter how well qualified. With the increasing substitution of banks and other institutions as trustees in place of trusted and respected family friends, and with the increasing complexity of the knowledge a competent investment manager may need and consequent specialization of investment managers, delegation is now permitted subject to safeguards. These include care in selecting the delegate, defining the delegate's duty, and monitoring the delegate's actions.

In the modern version of the rule, there is no reference to people managing their own affairs: Today, most money is under management by professionals rather than people acting directly for their own accounts. Further, there is a requirement that the fiduciary act in the manner of those familiar with such matters—a degree of expertise not required in the original version of the rule. Obviously, no one is expert in all aspects of financial matters, so the increased emphasis on professionalism and expertise may require a prudent expert, not just a prudent investor. In fact, under the modern rule, the pension fund trustee must delegate to an expert those areas of investment with which he or she may not be sufficiently familiar. As a simple example, the management of the stock portion of a portfolio might be delegated to an equity manager, and the management of the bond portion of the portfolio might be delegated to a fixed-income manager.

The task of this team of experts managing a pension fund or private trust is to strike a proper balance in the trade-off between risk and return. In the past, legislatures tried to specify those investments that are safe enough for trustees in long "legal lists" of particular investments that are permitted or prohibited. For example, public utility bonds of a certain credit rating might be permitted, and shares of mining companies might be prohibited. While this approach is still in some use today, particularly with regard to the investment of government funds, it has been replaced in pension fund investment by the more general prudent-investor test.

Role of Diversification: Portfolio Theory

The new ALI restatement of the prudent-investor rule also removes all categoric restrictions on the types of investments a trustee may make. The trustee can invest in anything that plays an appropriate role in achieving the risk/return objectives of the trust and that meets the other requirements of prudent investing. Moreover, the standard of prudence is applied to the portfolio as a whole, rather than to individual investments. This is in contrast to earlier rules, which examined each investment by itself and might have held a fiduciary liable for losses on that investment despite much greater successes in other investments. The modern rule recognizes that if a trustee has constructed a prudently diversified portfolio which produces a successful overall performance, the failure of a few investments should be disregarded in the overall context of success. In some cases, risks become losses; in other cases they do not, and taking them leads to rewards.

Diversification has always been recognized as an important component of prudent investing, but the intellectual underpinning for the renewed emphasis on diversification, and for the changes in the prudent-investor rules just discussed, has come from academic developments in portfolio theory, the efficient-market hypothesis, and the capital asset pricing model.

Today, pension fund managers typically develop a strategic asset allocation in which the portfolio investments are divided among asset classes whose price changes have historically not been highly correlated with one another. The bulk of such a portfolio might consist of a variety of stocks and bonds of U.S. companies, with the remainder including more risky investments, such as real estate, venture capital funds, stocks and bonds of other industrialized countries, and emerging markets. While some of the latter might be regarded as very risky, speculative, and volatile, they also offer the chance of producing very high returns. Chances are that when some of the very volatile investments are down, others will be up, so that the performance of the portfolio as a whole will be relatively smooth, particularly since the very volatile investments do not constitute a large percentage of the portfolio.

The composition of such a portfolio is quite different from that of portfolios considered acceptable in the past. The stock of U.S. companies is now considered a relatively conservative element of the portfolio. In the past, stocks were considered inappropriate investments for trusts, and condemned as speculation. As recently as 1934, a New Jersey court declared: "The stock market is not a playground for trustees. The ethics of trusteeship is not to be found in the code of the speculator. An executor's function is to conserve, not to venture. It is no less a breech of trust to speculate with securities of an estate than to gamble with the money, though the motive be to advance its interests." The standards of trustees have done a complete about-face in this regard, so that *failure to invest* in stocks may now be considered imprudent. In 1986, a

Washington court held a bank trustee liable for imprudent investing by failing to include stocks in a portfolio otherwise composed
entirely of tax-free bonds.

Duty to Use Derivatives

In short, the legal standards for prudent investing have evolved
right along with the standards of conduct in the financial community. In recent years, the largest single change in the financial community has been the emergence of trillions of dollars' worth of
derivatives traded on international over-the-counter markets as
well as regulated futures exchanges. Given the flexibility of the
prudent-investor rule—its regard for the conduct of others in the
financial community—future courts may well require the prudent
use of derivatives in a portfolio, just as the Washington court
required the prudent use of stocks. Legal obstacles to the use of
derivatives may be transformed into legal requirements for their
use. If hedging may sometimes be required in a corporate context,
as in the case of *Brane v. Roth*, it is even more likely to be required
in the context of pension and trust fiduciaries, who are held to
the higher standard of the prudent-investor rule rather than
the broader latitude allowed to corporate managers under the
business-judgment rule.

14

Standard of Care in Delegation

INTRODUCTION

If the prudent use of derivatives is to be permitted or even sometimes required under the law, the practice of delegation becomes especially critical. Few trustees have the expertise required for the prudent use of derivatives, and even the delegation of this function is a task that must be approached with great care. The complexity of derivatives, their volatility, and the potential for financial exposure far beyond the sums directly committed all require careful attention to the matter.

The standard of care in delegation requires attention to three basic elements: selection of the expert, instruction of the expert, and monitoring of the expert. Each of the three is of critical importance.

GENERAL SELECTION OF EXPERTS

Selection of an expert by pension fiduciaries typically involves a search with the help of a consultant. Various consulting firms make it their business to know the specialties of particular investment managers, as well as their track records and reputations. These consultants compile databases that also permit the comparison of investment managers in a particular specialty.

The file on a particular manager may include reports on conversations during visits by the manager to the consultant's office, visits by the consultants to the manager's office to observe the environment in which the manager works, an analysis of the resources that appear to be available to the manager, as well as statistical and analytical reports on the manager and its track record (which may include reports by the manager's independent auditor).

Based on this kind of research, the consultant can provide the pension fiduciary with a list of candidates who have the expertise to handle the particular investment specialty that the fiduciary wishes to delegate. The pension fiduciary making the delegation is usually represented in this regard by a committee. In the case of a law firm pension plan, for example, the committee may consist of partners from various offices of the law firm who may have some knowledge of investment matters or who may simply be considered representative of the partners as a group. In the case of a corporation, the committee would ordinarily consist of corporate personnel with financial expertise, as well as some representatives who have particular knowledge of employee needs and attitudes.

The committee, together with the consultants, will then meet with candidates for the particular task and form an impression of the manager's expertise and understanding of the client's objectives. They must then select one of the candidates for the task, or perhaps more than one if the funds allocated to the managers are sufficiently large and if there is a desire to create a competitive environment among two or more managers.

This sort of selection process is designed to ensure that the managers selected are well qualified for their task, and also that the process itself displays enough diligence and prudence so that any future judge or jury will conclude that the selection of the manager was not lightly or carelessly done—even if the manager later fails in its task.

When it comes to selecting derivatives managers, few consultants have built the kind of databases and files just described, although some have begun to do so. Of course, fiduciaries can select managers without the help of a consultant, but it is more difficult to judge the capability of an expert without the advice of another expert. This need might be met by retaining an investment bank with a substantial derivatives business to advise the fiduciary on the selection of other derivatives managers, disqualifying the advisory investment bank from recommending itself for the job.

INSTRUCTION OF THE EXPERT

Once the manager has been selected, proper instruction of the manager is also critical. Since the manager is being hired for a particular expertise, he or she will not ordinarily be familiar with every aspect of the portfolio. Instead, the manager will be allocated a small portion of the portfolio and will be judged upon handling that portion, whether the balance of the portfolio prospers or not.

For example, a manager charged with investing a portion of the portfolio in stocks of large corporations considered to be "value" investments will be judged against the portfolio of other managers and mutual funds with a similar strategy, and not against the performance of another manager of the portfolio's funds that has been assigned the specialty of investing in the stocks of small, rapidly growing corporations. It is the overall portfolio manager who decides the overall *strategic asset allocation:* How much of the portfolio funds should be allocated to the first type of manager, how much to the second, and how much to other types. In making this allocation, the overall portfolio manager must not only consider the individual performance of the different managers, but the historical correlation between the different styles of the managers. If large value stocks are not highly correlated with small growth stocks, then the overall performance of the portfolio may be less volatile, since both types of investments are not as likely to fall in value at the same time.

Having selected a manager for a particular area of expertise, the fiduciary responsible for the overall portfolio will want to be sure that the manager stays within his or her defined area. The written instructions to the manager should make it very clear what the expected area of investment should be. If the instructions given to the large value manager and small growth manager are too vague, both may end up investing in the same stocks, and the benefits of diversification in styles and strategies will be lost. The two parts of the portfolio will be highly correlated with one another, rather than uncorrelated as the overall fiduciary had hoped.

SELECTION OF DERIVATIVE EXPERTS

The same principles apply in the selection of derivative managers. However, two considerations unique to the derivative area require special attention.

First, the use of derivatives often involves leverage, so the exposure in the derivatives portion of the portfolio must be considered in light of the size and liquidity of the overall portfolio. For example, if $10 million is assigned to a derivatives manager, the manager might use the funds to make commitments with total face values of $100 million, against which a $5 million deposit will be required. If the face value of the commitment falls by 20 percent, this would entail a paper loss of $20 million, and additional margin deposits of $20 million might be required. Since the derivative manager was allocated only $10 million initially, he or she will be forced to either liquidate the position or request an additional $15 million of other plan assets to maintain it. If the position is liquidated, the manager will have lost not only the initial $10 million, but another $10 million in value of assets that must come from some other source. Even if the position is maintained in the hope that it will recoup its lost value, this can be done only by providing the manager with an additional $15 million in cash to meet the margin call—cash that must also be obtained from other portfolio assets not originally allocated to this manager.

In short, the risks associated with leverage must always be considered when allocating funds to a derivatives manager, and the instructions given to that manager should explicitly take account of this risk. If there is a possibility that adverse market moves could involve loss of funds in excess of those committed to the manager or that there may be margin calls requiring additional funds, these possibilities should be recognized and provided for by defining the extent of additional funds that could be made available. As an added incentive to avoid unanticipated losses, the effects of such a loss on the managers compensation, continued employment, or liability might also be made explicit.

Another way to limit the risk of leverage is to instruct the manager that he or she may undertake commitments in excess of authorized funds only by purchasing options. In this way, the derivatives trader might undertake commitments totaling $100 million with a worst-case exposure to the portfolio of less than $10 million. Of course, the cost of nonrecourse leverage in the form of options is the time premium paid for the options. Another alternative is to instruct the manager that the portfolio must be liquidated if the losses ever reach $5 million, or half of the funds entrusted to that manager. This method of limiting losses is, however, not completely reliable. If the market falls rapidly, losses could exceed the target amount before the trader is able to take action. On one day in October 1987, for example, the stock market fell so rapidly that it would have been impossible to restrict the loss on the value of a $100 million stock portfolio to anything approaching 5 percent, or $5 million. Obviously, these are issues that need to be carefully considered and addressed in the instructions given the manager.

Once again, remember that a leveraged investment is not necessarily bad or excessively risky. The risks associated with a $100 million commitment by a manager allocated only $10 million might be acceptable when taken by an overall portfolio of $10 billion, for which even $100 million is only 1 percent of the total portfolio. These risks would be an entirely different matter, however, for a portfolio totaling only $40 million dollars, where losses by this derivative trader entrusted with $10 million, or one-fourth of the portfolio, could conceivably result in the loss of the entire portfolio.

SPECIAL CONSIDERATIONS OF DERIVATIVES USED AS A HEDGE

The second area in which derivatives differ from other asset allocations lies in their hedging capabilities: their potential to reduce risk. This relates to the fact that derivatives are not themselves an asset class in the way that stocks or bonds are defined as asset classes, but instead are a form of investment applicable to many different asset classes, including stocks and bonds, and as such may interrelate with many other elements of the portfolio. As an example, a derivatives manager who is allocated $10 million to trade financial futures might be judged on profits generated from his or her trading activities, in absolute dollar and percentage terms, and also in comparison to other financial futures traders. However, there is an additional dimension to the manager's activity that may be of considerable importance to the portfolio as a whole. For example, most portfolios include substantial investments in bonds. If the derivatives trader is long in bond market futures, this in effect increases the overall allocation of the portfolio to bonds, meaning greater profits if the bond market rises and greater losses if the bond market falls. If the derivatives trader is short in bonds, on the other hand, this decreases the exposure of the portfolio to the bond market. In that case, if the bond market rises the portfolio's net gain will be smaller, and if it falls the portfolio's loss will be less than if the derivative trader were not making these investments.

For this reason, the correlation of the derivative trader's activities with the other elements of the portfolio must be carefully considered in the instructions given to the trader. For example, the trader may be instructed to take only positions that are short in the bond market, not long. In this way, the overall portfolio manager will be assured that the derivative trader's activity will act only as a hedge against the bond investments elsewhere in the portfolio and will not increase the portfolio's exposure to the bond market. If the derivatives trader can still turn a profit with the limitation imposed by this instruction, then he or she will not only be turning a profit on those funds, but will also be decreasing the portfolio's risk from its bond investments elsewhere, since the derivatives position taken may from time to time act as a hedge against those investments. The hedge will not be perfect or continuous, since there will be times when the trader will be out of the market, expecting bond prices to rise. Nevertheless, if the trader's activities are successful, this instruction will have made them doubly successful by producing a profit not only from the derivative trading activity, but also by decreasing the volatility and loss exposure of the portfolio as a whole.

Again, these sorts of considerations must be carefully taken into account in formulating the instructions for derivatives managers as part of the overall strategy of the portfolio. Indeed, the derivative manager, more than other sorts of managers, may be useful in providing an overview of the portfolio as a whole by identifying those matters in which derivative trading activity may produce hedging benefits beyond the profit of the trading activity itself. The complexity of these matters may, however, be such that the portfolio would benefit from consulting advice from a derivatives expert who is independent from the derivative manager. In other words, an independent expert might be called upon to help formulate the instructions to the derivatives trader.

MONITORING THE EXPERT MANAGER

Once the manager has been carefully selected and instructed, the fiduciary must take care to monitor the manager on a continuing basis to ensure that the manager is staying within the scope of the instructions given, and that those instructions remain appropriate. The ease and confidence with which this monitoring function can be carried out depends in part on the organization or structure within which the investment was made. For example, if an independent organization has custody of the funds and investments that the manager has made, reports from that outside organization provide an independent source of information. Similarly, futures commission merchants maintain custody of the investments made by commodity trading advisers and can provide daily reports on the activity, contents, and value of the account, as well as margin requirements. Bank custodians also often keep custody of stocks or bonds purchased by investment managers, and of the funds in the investment manager's control. In the case of over-the-counter derivatives, custody of the asset is in effect maintained by the counterparty to the transaction, so that this sort of independent information source is unavailable. However, regular reports can be requested from the manager or the counterparty, and periodic audits can confirm the information provided.

Whatever the mechanism adopted for monitoring, the volatility and risks associated with high leverage require greater attention than that accorded to unleveraged stock and bond portfolios. Often, such portfolios are reviewed by a pension committee on a quarterly basis only, well after the end of the quarter being reviewed. In such a case, a member of the committee is usually designated to review the investments on at least a monthly basis and to call a meeting of the committee in the event of extraordinary circumstances. A quarterly review well after the end of the quarter may be too infrequent in the derivatives markets, depending on the instructions given the trader and the financial resources of the trader to make good any unauthorized losses.

Even if the derivatives are not highly leveraged, closer monitoring may still be called for because of the interrelationship between derivative activity and the other parts of the portfolio, including their potential use as a hedge. Pension plans such as the Virginia Retirement System and the San Diego County Employees Retirement System have retained trading advisers to monitor managed futures accounts on a daily basis. In fact, in these cases, several levels of monitoring were provided.

First, the actual traders were not given custody of the funds or contracts themselves, but were only authorized to trade them through an independent futures commissions merchant, who provided reports on all trading activity on a daily or even intradaily basis. Second, the consultants who had advised the pension funds in the selection of the traders were themselves retained to monitor the traders on a daily basis, and were directed to withdraw the funds from the traders if they thought that this was advisable. Third, another consultant was retained who was not involved in the selection or instruction of the traders. This consultant was instructed to (1) receive daily reports from traders and futures commissions merchants, (2) track the investments on a continuous basis to ensure that they remained within the guidelines, and (3) advise liquidation of the positions under defined circumstances.

Such measures involve costs, but they may be well worth every penny. In each instance, of course, the costs of this continuous monitoring must be considered as an attribute of the investment in addition to the risks and rewards offered by the investment.

15

Legal Liability in Using Derivatives

BUYER'S AUTHORITY TO BUY

Authority of Trader

Who is responsible for determining whether a particular derivative transaction is suitable for a particular investor? As we have discussed, the investor may or may not be sophisticated in investment matters in general or in derivatives investments in particular. Even if an investor has some familiarity with derivative investments, he or she may or may not be expert in the particular derivative in question and its relationship to the rest of the portfolio. If the investment goes awry, the investor may argue that it is the fault of the counterparty or derivative trader for selling an investment unsuited to the investor's needs. The investor went to an expert in the field because of the expert's greater knowledge of derivatives, and may argue that the dealer therefore had a responsibility to sell a safe derivative.

While the counterparty or trader may be sophisticated with regard to derivatives and with regard to the particular derivative in question, they may have no knowledge of the portfolio in which this particular derivative investment is being placed. Indeed, the investor may wish to keep all of that information private. Certainly, the investor is unlikely to ask the other party to every transaction for a complete analysis of the investor's portfolio, its history, objectives, liquidity needs, and other factors that may be relevant to a correct evaluation of the derivative investment. Even if the investor were to ask for this sort of analysis, it would require considerable work, and there would probably be a substantial fee involved. The investor can hardly ask for this kind of analysis for each derivative transaction. Accordingly, the seller of the derivatives may reasonably resist assuming responsibility in any way for the use the investor actually makes of the derivatives, or for its suitability for the investor's portfolio.

Much of the recent outpouring of litigation over derivatives has revolved around this sort of question of relative responsibility of the parties for a particular derivative investment. While the law on this subject is still emerging, and will not be fully settled until a number of courts, and perhaps legislatures, have spoken on the subject, it may well develop along lines suggested by precedents established in other areas of the law. In the meantime, the parties to the transaction may benefit from spelling out their expectations of each other beforehand, rather than go to the courts later.

Buyer's Authority to Buy

A central issue in a derivative investment is the question whether the party making the investment has the authority to make it at all. This is an important issue for both the buyer and seller of the investment, since if the buyer does not have the authority to make the investment, the seller may be required to take back the investment and return any consideration paid for it. If the investment has changed in value in the meanwhile this can be a very problematical state of affairs.

This issue has been the basis of several lawsuits by organizations attempting to repudiate the actions of their officers or other employees. The outcome of the litigation often turns on the reasonableness of the seller's conduct. If it was a transaction in the ordinary course of business of the investor, of the kind frequently done by other similar investors and by this investor in the past, even a lower-ranking employee might be considered to have "apparent authority" to enter the transaction, whether or not that employee had actually been given such authority within his or her organization. If a reasonable person, from all the circumstances, would have thought that the particular representative of the organization had authority to make the investment, then the investing organization will be held to the investment even if the official had never actually been given the authority to make it. On the other hand, if the investment was of an unusual type and of a large size in relation to the investor organization, then the seller of the investment might be expected to ask the investing official for some evidence of authority to make the investment. For example, the seller might ask for a copy of meeting minutes of the board of directors of the organization or of a duly constituted committee of the board, authorizing the particular investment or enabling the particular official to make investments of this type. Such a resolution of the board, certified by the secretary of the corporation, would provide the seller with good protection against later attempts to repudiate the sale.

Any investor organization should consider the adoption of specific, written policies to specify the size and type of derivative investments that can be made and the personnel authorized to make them. Even if such a policy will not protect against reasonable investments made by a representative of the company, it could still avoid expensive mistakes within the organization. It will also provide comfort to outside parties looking for evidence of authority to invest. As for people likely to be in positions of apparent authority, internal controls need to be developed to ensure they do not make investments beyond their actual authority.

Ultra Vires

Even if it is clear that a particular official has been authorized by the organization to make the investment, a sale of the investment may still not be entirely free from the risk of repudiation. The organization itself may be prohibited from making the investment by applicable laws or regulations, however much its officials may think that they have the power to make the investment. Such investments are described as *ultra vires*, or beyond the power of the organization.

Such a situation arose in England when a number of local governmental bodies began making derivative investments. They purchased investments, they paid for them, and when the investments lost value, they tried to repudiate their investments on the grounds that they were beyond the legal authority of the governmental unit under English law. The matter was litigated all the way to the House of Lords, which decided that the purchases were indeed beyond the power of the governmental units and that the plaintiffs were entitled to recoup their losses. This same issue has also arisen in the United States, under the laws of West Virginia and California, where two cases making the same claims are now in the process of litigation.

The risk of repudiation of a transaction is typically greater in the case of a governmental body than it is when the investor is a private corporation. It would be an unusual corporation whose articles and bylaws or governing corporate law prohibited investment in derivatives. Nevertheless, if a seller of derivatives is obtaining a certificate from the corporate secretary of the investor attesting to the power of the individual to make the investment, it may do well to ask for additional certification that the investment is authorized under the articles and bylaws of the corporation and all rules and regulations applicable to the corporation. In the case of some highly regulated investors, such as banks, insurance companies, or utilities, it is possible that statutory law or regulations may limit their investment powers.

Conclusion

It is important for both buyers and sellers of derivatives to understand their respective responsibilities so that each will not think that an important decision issue is being taken care of by the other. The losses and litigation that can result from such a mistake can overwhelm in importance any temporary advantage which a party may think is available from glossing over these issues.

SUITABILITY OF DERIVATIVE INVESTMENTS

If the seller of a derivative product knows more about the investment, and the buyer of the derivative product knows more about the portfolio into which it must fit, the determination that a particular derivative investment is suitable for a particular portfolio depends upon the knowledge of both parties. However, the issue of legal responsibility for the decision is unlikely to arise unless losses result from it and a lawsuit is filed or threatened. In such a lawsuit, there are a variety of claims an investor might make against those who sold the investment.

Fraud

Fraud is the strongest claim, if the facts bear it out. To prove fraud, however, the investor must show that the defendant *knowingly* misstated a fact that was *material*. The investor must also show that he or she relied on the misstatement in entering the transaction, and that this *reliance* was *reasonable*. Reliance on the misstatement might be considered unreasonable if the investor had other information suggesting that the defendant's statement was untrue, or could easily have uncovered such information. If the investor can prove all of these elements of fraud, the investor has a good claim under most state fraud laws, and also under federal law if the sale involved a security.

Omissions

The investor has a somewhat weaker case where the defendant has not actually misstated a material fact, but has simply failed to disclose to the investor an important fact known to the defendant. Despite old notions of *caveat emptor,* or buyer beware, sellers run a risk when they withhold information important to the investors with whom they deal. Even so, if the undisclosed fact was something the investor could easily have found out, courts are less likely to hold the defendant liable than in the case of an actual misstatement.

Furthermore, investing fiduciaries may themselves be in trouble for claiming that those who sold the derivative product should have revealed certain things about it. The defendants may show that this knowledge was readily available, and that they had reasonably assumed the investors were already aware of it. Proof of these facts would lay the investing fiduciaries open to a suit by the other people whose money they were managing on the grounds of breach of fiduciary obligation to *them* by failing to use due care in making the investment, whatever the seller might have done or said. The investing fiduciary may prefer to avoid the spotlight of litigation altogether.

In the previous discussion, we have assumed that the seller was aware of some fact and either misrepresented it to the investor (a strong case for liability) or simply failed to disclose it to the investor (a weaker case). Sometimes, however, the investor may claim that the seller *should have known* of such a fact and disclosed it to the investor. This is a harder case for the investor to establish, but still not impossible. The investor must prove the seller was reckless in not finding out about the fact. One court defined this recklessness as behavior that was "highly unreasonable and such an extreme departure from the standard of ordinary care as to present a danger of misleading the plaintiff to the extent that the danger was either known to the defendant or so obvious that the defendant must have been aware of it." This standard is difficult to meet, and leaves the plaintiff investors open to the reply that if the danger was so obvious, the fiduciary investor should have discovered it for themselves.

Proof of liability is easier under some sections of the securities laws, which do not require that the investor prove reliance upon the statements made or omitted, but only that there was a misstatement or omission of a material fact. These strict liability standards apply only to a narrow class of investments where a security is issued; they usually do not apply to exchange-traded derivatives or to many types of over-the-counter derivatives or currency forwards.

FIDUCIARY DUTIES AND SUITABILITY

SEC Requirements

Up to this point, we have assumed that the investor is dealing at arm's length with the party selling the derivative product. In such a case, the investor has a right to assume that the seller will not misstate material facts, or even withhold material information, at least where that information is not readily available to the investor.

The investor's case is much stronger, however, when the investors have reason to believe that the parties are not dealing at arm's length; that is, when the investors believe that they can rely upon the other party for advice as well as for the sale of a product. The investors may believe that the buyer has undertaken the role of their adviser or their agent, or otherwise occupies a position enjoying the trust and confidence of the investor. In such a situation, the seller may have fiduciary duties to protect buyers from their own ignorance or carelessness.

When an investor buys derivatives from a stockbroker, he or she probably expects that a broker has such an obligation. The SEC has found that once a broker "hangs out a shingle," the implication to customers is that the broker will deal with them fairly and in accordance with the standards and practices of the profession. Some state courts have explicitly found that "the relationship between broker and principal is fiduciary in nature and imposes a . . . duty of acting in the highest good faith toward the principal." Another court held that "there is in all cases a fiduciary duty owed by a stockbroker to his or her customers; the scope of this duty depends on the specific facts and circumstances in a given case." However, the California court making this observation also noted that federal courts find a fiduciary duty only if the broker has "continuing control over the customer's account or acts as an 'investment counselor.' "

Product Liability Law Analogy

Many sellers of derivatives are not broker-dealers regulated under the federal securities law. They may be banks regulated by the Comptroller of the Currency, futures commission merchants regulated by the CFTC, insurance companies subject to state regulators, or corporate entities subject to none of these regulations. In these cases, the existence of a fiduciary duty will depend on all the facts and circumstances.

Of course, if there is a fiduciary duty, the parties are no longer dealing at arm's length, and the investor can rely upon the other party to fulfill its duties of loyalty and care toward the investor. These duties impose a much higher standard than those of fraudulent misrepresentation or omission applicable between parties negotiating at arm's length. However, the existence and scope of these duties as they apply to derivatives is subject to much conjecture, since the courts have as yet decided few such cases.

One analogous area of law that has developed over many years is that of product liability. One of the principles of product liability law is that there is "an implied warranty of fitness for a particular purpose" if the seller has reason to know that the buyer intends to use the merchandise for a particular purpose and the buyer is relying upon the seller's skill and judgment in selecting the merchandise. Sellers often disclaim such obligations. For example, everyone has seen warnings such as the following:

Seller makes no warranty of any kind, express or implied, concerning the use of this product. Buyer assumes all risk in use or handling, whether in accord with directions or not.

Disclaimers such as these must be in writing and conspicuous, set out in red, for example, or in boldface type. Even so, they do not provide complete protection for the seller.

In product liability cases, results often depend upon the relative sophistication of the buyer and the seller and the reasonable expectations of each as to what the other party knows and should disclose. Between sophisticated commercial parties, these expectations are frequently set out in writing, and the written document is very important in resolving any later disputes.

Such disclaimers should not necessarily be frowned upon. Parties to derivative transactions are almost always sophisticated businesspeople and business entities, not individual consumers. They may therefore find it more practical and efficient to deal at arm's length. The Federal Reserve Board of New York has embodied this idea in a draft, "Wholesale Transactions Code of Conduct," which states in part that parties to derivative transactions should assume that "each counterparty deals at arm's length for its own account." But this code also provides that a seller should "evaluate its counterparty's capability to understand and make independent decisions." If one party determines the other to be lacking in that capability, the transaction should be refused, or there should be a written agreement of disclosures and disclaimers.

Apart from any written agreement, courts will consider each party's sophistication and expertise with respect to the particular product being purchased, its access to information about the product, which party initiated the transaction, and which party developed the specifications for the product. These determinations will not necessarily be easy or straightforward.

Aside from the kinds of doctrines discussed earlier in the chapter, investors have no clear right to expect those who sell them derivative products to make a determination that the particular product is suitable for a particular investor's portfolio. The CFTC, which has exclusive jurisdiction over futures, does not require futures brokers to determine the suitability of their customers investments, nor have bank regulators imposed this requirement on all banks selling derivatives. Banks, combined with presently unregulated corporations selling derivatives, are by far the largest sources of derivative products. Broker-dealers registered with the SEC, a much smaller source of derivative products, are required to know their customers under the rules of the New York Stock Exchange and the NASD. NASD also requires brokers to sell only suitable investments. However, none of these regulations give the investor a right to sue. If the regulations are breached, the only remedy is a disciplinary proceeding by the regulator.

CONCLUSION

The law's present lack of clarity on these matters makes it even more important for those with supervisory responsibility for derivatives in an organization to clearly define and limit the scope of responsibility of each individual in the process, including everyone within the organization—from the board of directors to the trader executing the trades. They should also define their expectations from all of those outside parties with whom the organization deals. Once this is done, a system for monitoring performance can be designed so that actions outside the scope of this authority can be identified early enough to prevent serious losses. Clear policies and tight controls can prevent disasters. Finger-pointing after the fact has proved of little value to the supervisors, chief executives, and directors who have been subjected to career damage and litigation as a result of losses incurred by unknown subordinates.

16

Looking Forward

In this book we have attempted to give the reader a broad overview of the derivatives landscape. We have zoomed in for more detailed discussions in some areas but by and large have kept away from a technical discussion of products. Our objective was to provide a perspective that would allow you to identify the issues that you find important and to develop a viewpoint based on a fuller appreciation of the dimensions of this important market.

Looking to the future, one might ask how this marketplace will develop. What will be the new products or applications? Where will we be in terms of regulation and oversight? Will the risk of a system meltdown increase? In the following paragraphs we consider the future. This is speculation and not prediction.

Derivatives are here to stay. Derivatives represent a process of dealing with the relative value and connectivity between different markets. This technology allows a participant to evaluate alternative investments, transform liabilities and assets, restructure portfolios, and deal with the connections between different markets. It connects global capital markets geographically and connects each individual market with itself over time with the future. For example, derivatives allow us to connect, and therefore make business commitments and investments, based on the relative value between the German bond market and the U.S. bond market. Similarly, they allow us to connect, and therefore make business commitments and investments, based on the relative value between current rates and forward or future rates within the U.S. bond market.

If we place derivatives within the context of macro forces around us it is easy to see why we believe that derivatives are here to stay. There are two things we can say with great confidence about the developing financial markets of tomorrow. First, financial markets have an increasing degree of complexity. Second, they are increasingly interconnected globally. They may also be increasingly volatile. If this is so, it is clear that derivatives will continue to play an important and growing role in the marketplace.

Derivatives and Investing

Much of the news in this area during the past year has been related to the debacles surrounding losses, including those suffered by several state and municipal pension funds. These were important landmarks in the evolution of the marketplace. However, these losses were actually very small in relation to the total volume of derivative use for investing, and were often avoidable by application of the principles explained in this book.

Currently, derivatives are used by many investment committees to hedge risks, leverage investments, and create investment structures that are not otherwise readily available. The use of derivatives for hedging will continue to grow exponentially, both in terms of volume and numbers of users. As financial markets become more complex and volatile, this seems almost inevitable.

The use of derivatives to create leverage is a different proposition. Derivatives do provide an efficient mechanism for leverage. However, as these instruments are better understood by investment managers, regulators, and credit agencies, their use to create leverage will be examined more carefully. Although this usage will grow with the overall growth in financial flows, we do not see it growing exponentially. After all, there is nothing new in leverage. The good and the bad that leverage represents has been known for a long time. There will always be surges in leverage activity when markets are going up and there will be debacles and even catastrophes when they change direction. Derivatives will be used or not used based on efficiency. As participants become more knowledge-able, the use of derivatives to create leverage where leverage is nei-ther permitted nor appropriate will and should be restricted.

The use of derivatives and financial engineering to create investment structures not readily available in the marketplace is an interesting area for conjecture. Our view is that these invest-ment structures will continue to proliferate and grow in an expo-nential manner. This will be driven by two factors. First, as the global financial markets become more integrated and as invest-ment officers are further challenged to outperform the average, discrepancies in relative values between markets around the world and between asset classes will be exploited more and more fully. This is usually hard to do by using readily available cash instruments and requires some derivatives-based financial engi-neering. As a simple example, an investor might study the ratio of the S&P Index to the Long Bond Index, decide that it is trading too far above or below its usual range, and wish to invest money with the view that the ratio will revert back to its normal range. This trade can easily be made in the public futures or options markets after calculating appropriate ratios, but a similar trade between the U.S. dollar–pound sterling exchange rate and the U.K. stock market would require a specially designed private contract. Such cross-market correlation constitutes a vast new area that remains to be developed.

The second factor that will cause specialized investment struc-tures to grow and proliferate is technology. By technology we mean financial engineering as well as computer and information processing technology: hardware and software. The development of the mathematics of financial engineering is progressing by leaps and bounds; simultaneously, the ability to transmit informa-tion in real time and to manipulate large amounts of data on fast computers results in ever-newer trading strategies. This trading activity results in an ability to establish prices on new combina-tions of financial parameters, and these in turn lead to the creation of more and more fine-tuned products tailored to specific user needs. We see these trends continuing in the near future.

Derivatives and the Individual
Individuals use derivatives in two different ways: (1) *directly*, through products and services they buy, and (2) *indirectly*, through

investments in mutual funds and pension funds that use derivatives. Mutual funds and pension funds use all the techniques discussed in the preceding paragraphs. Direct individual use of derivatives is now more limited, but new ways may emerge for individuals to use derivatives directly in the coming years. It is not necessary nor is it always possible for individuals to understand all the technical details behind the construction of a product that uses derivatives. Two analogies will serve to make this point. First, take the case of the family car. The users know what it is for, how to operate it, how not to operate it, and so forth. Very few users, however, know how the internal combustion engine works or how transmissions are put together. Second, take the case of the home mortgage. Most homeowners have seen and used mortgages with periodic caps, lifetime caps, and similar features. They know, or ought to know, how the interest rate on their mortgage will be set and what happens to it if one of the cap rates are hit. However, very few people know how caps (or options) are priced, hedged, or traded by derivatives traders.

It is possible that within the next three to five years, banks could provide a range of derivative-based investment options: perhaps even through ATMs. For example, a person could stop at the corner ATM and transfer funds into a principal-protected S&P 500 fund. The principal invested would not fall below par for the period of the investment, say six months, and the investor would have an upside appreciation opportunity linked to the performance of the S&P 500 index. The derivatives technology as well as the network technology for such a product already exists. Obviously, a number of regulatory and other issues need to be addressed before such a product can be offered, but they are far from insurmountable.

Another possibility would be for individuals to use their ATMs to invest in various asset classes and to balance or rebalance their portfolios as they wish. Instead of picking specific stocks and bond investments, an individual would invest in indexes that represent broad sectors of the market. For example, an investor could go to an ATM and invest 50 percent of his or her funds in the S&P index and 50 percent in the XYZ government bond index. Having done that, the investor could, whenever he or she desires, change the allocation between the two asset classes by spending a few minutes at the ATM.

Turning from investments to borrowing, one idea would be for individuals to borrow money against owned assets on a matched basis. For example, an individual might borrow money against owned real estate such that the principal repayment would be based on a real estate index. If real estate prices went up, the repayment on the loan would go up, and vice versa. The owner of the real estate would, therefore, have his or her assets and liabilities partially matched or hedged. Another example of this concept would be a matched borrowing using a portfolio of securities owned by the borrower. In a standard margin loan, the borrower uses the portfolio as collateral, but the borrowing is not matched in any way to the price performance of the portfolio. It is conceivable that banks might lend money against portfolios where the repayment amount of the loan is linked to the price performance of the portfolio. This would be helpful to the borrower as well as the lender. The borrower would have a partial hedge on his or her loan and the lender would be better off from the point of view of its credit exposure, since the loan and the collateral would be linked in terms of sensitivity to market value changes.

The market is evolving so quickly that it is even possible that the ideas discussed here will have seen the light of day by the time this book reaches the bookstore.

Derivatives and Systemic Risk

Derivative transactions, either directly or indirectly, involve counterparty contracts for settlement in the future. Because of this, there is always some kind of counterparty credit risk involved. The derivatives market currently consists of contracts worth many trillions of dollars between millions of counterparties. The question is whether the financial system has a greater risk of disruption and failure because of this fact.

The risk of failure or disruption of a system is based on two factors. At the micro level is the risk of failure of individual entities within the system. At the macro level is the risk of the system failing because of the connectivity between individual units. Those who fear collapse of the system theorize that because of the dense universe of counterparty connections, a failure in one part of the system will be transmitted rapidly throughout the system and, therefore, lead to a greater breakdown.

We feel that the development of the derivatives market and the risk analysis and risk management techniques associated with it can actually reduce the risk of disruption and failure of individual institutions. It is quite likely that there will be individual instances of institutions that are more risky because of derivatives. However, by and large, the ability to understand different kinds of risks, to measure them and to mitigate them, has improved considerably due to the development of derivatives.

A simple example is that of banks and other lending institutions. Until very recently, the overall interest rate risk or mismatch in the loan portfolios of banks was analyzed and managed in very rudimentary fashion. There has always been interest rate risk to banks because they borrow from depositors on a short-term basis and lend to borrowers on a longer-term basis. Banks are very highly leveraged, so this risk is substantial, even without derivatives. Indeed, the entire savings and loan industry in the United States was threatened with bankruptcy when short-term interest rates paid depositors soared in the early 1980s while interest collected from homeowners on long-term, fixed-rate loans remained constant.

Before the development of derivatives, even the most sophisticated institutions used very simple gap analysis to get a picture of their asset liability mismatch. The swap business, on the other hand, uses rigorous mark-to-market procedures to value the mismatch between cash inflows and outflows or between assets and liabilities. Over time, as concern over swap portfolios grew, practitioners and regulators realized that the interest rate mismatch they were concerned about actually applies to the entire asset/ liability portfolio of the institution, and that the mathematics and procedures used in the analysis of risk and pricing in the derivatives market could be applied to the analysis of risk at the company level. The concept of using value at risk to evaluate and manage overall risk in derivatives portfolios is now being used as a foundation for risk management at the corporate level in financial institutions and as a measuring tool for regulators who oversee markets.

As for risk to the system as a whole, this risk may actually be reduced rather than increased, because of the dense connectivity between institutions arising from derivatives contracts. It is hard to establish this point one way or the other by analytical methods based on empirical observations, but a theoretical argument supports the view that risk is reduced. In a general sense, there are two ways to look at structural integrity of systems. One is the theory of the weakest link, and the other is the theory of shock propagation. Under the *weakest link theory*, a system is as strong as the weakest link. Under the *shock propagation theory*, a system structure is weak if shocks are transmitted fully from one point to the other without damping.

The network of financial institutions connected through derivatives is linked together as a dense web. In such a system, the weakest link is usually strengthened by the network around it. The sturdiness of such a system depends on how quickly a shock in one place would be transmitted throughout the system and whether the system would damp the shock as it progressed. It is our observation that in the few instances where there has been a major disruption in one part of the system, the derivatives market has been able to damp the disturbance very effectively, such that the ripple effect did not move out of the immediate circle of counterparties. We have had the collapse of Drexel Burnham, which at that time had a derivatives portfolio of billions of dollars. We have had the collapse of Baring's, the Orange County imbroglio, and many other minor and major debacles. In all of these instances the system shocks have been absorbed very efficiently, with little or no ripple effect. One possible explanation is that the sheer size and denseness of the system helps in damping shocks arising out of individual disasters.

Derivatives and Regulation

In spite of the current wave of deregulation in the United States and around the world, it is safe to assume that over the next five years there will be more regulation and oversight of the derivatives market. Why is this so? Because of growth and because of complexity.

The derivatives market has grown tremendously in the last decade and increasing numbers of institutions and individuals are participating in this market, either directly or indirectly. Major universities are starting or planning programs in financial engineering. Accounting and legal firms are establishing departments to deal with derivatives. Lawmakers and politicians are hiring aides and specialists who understand derivatives. The derivatives business is so pervasive that it is being transformed from a segment of the financial markets to a process or mode of thinking that pervades all financial markets. So, growth in size and participants is almost inevitable.

As global financial markets become more integrated and as the ability to measure, isolate, and manage risk gets finer and finer, the complexity of transactions will continue to increase. As the size and complexity of the market grows and as it affects more and more entities, the social policy implications of the activity become larger. When this happens it is inevitable and understandable that regulators and lawmakers will focus their attention on this market.

It is not our intent to distinguish good regulation from bad regulation in this chapter. However, there are some general points that we would like to make. We feel that regulators should, broadly speaking, focus on three things: disclosure, consistency, and marking to market. We should try to achieve standard forms of disclosure so that the numbers presented convey the most information in the least ambiguous manner. We should have consistency in reporting between industries such as banks and insurance companies, and also between countries. And derivatives positions should be marked to market frequently, particularly when they involve high leverage, so that losses are not concealed until it is too late to cut them short without major trauma.

The issue of legal responsibility for the suitability of a particular derivative use is much more complex. The issue here is determining who bears the loss of other people's money when a derivative investment goes bad: (1) those other people (pension fund retirees, mutual fund investors, corporate shareholders, and the like), (2) the managers of their money, or (3) the people who sold a derivative product to those managers. As previously discussed in detail, existing law and precedents provide a good framework for answering these questions, even though few of the new cases involving derivatives have yet resulted in published judicial decisions. Differing standards for disclosure to sophisticated and unsophisticated investors already exist; and private contracts should (and we think will) develop to more clearly allocate responsibility for different aspects of derivative investment decisions between investors, their advisers, and those from whom investors purchase derivative investments. New legislation and regulation should focus on eliminating the confusion which arises from conflicting regulatory and legal frameworks covering a single product. As it stands now, for example, SEC, CFTC, banking, and insurance law all have different rules regarding a derivative product, which might be a security, a future, or a simple private contract. This goal need not be achieved by establishing a single network of rules and regulations that apply to every dealer and user of derivatives, which would probably be so complex as to be unworkable, but rather by clearly delineating existing regulatory boundaries in such a way that market participants can easily comply, without finding themselves overwhelmed by jurisdictional disputes among the regulators. The same sort of reform is needed on an international level, with each country providing clear rules concerning the enforceability of derivative contracts, so that derivatives can fulfill their role of interconnecting the capital markets of the world without the costs and systemic risks arising from uncertainty as to legal rights, responsibilities, and remedies.

Glossary

amortized loan A loan that is paid off in equal periodic payments. The payments are applied to principal and interest in varying portions over the life of the loan. The typical example is a home loan.

arbitrage The process of simultaneously purchasing in one market and selling in another a security or commodity in order to take advantage of price differences in the different markets.

asset allocation Process of dividing investment funds among different asset categories in such a way as to provide an optimal mix of risk and return.

backwardation Phenomenon where the current spot price of an item is higher than the current price for future delivery (i.e., the futures price).

Black-Scholes model A mathematical model used to determine the value of an option.

broker An agent who receives a commission for handling orders to buy and sell securities or futures contracts.

business-judgment rule A rule that allows corporate decision makers to do what they think is best for the corporation by immunizing them from liability. Under this rule, so long as the decision was a business decision, taken in good faith, without any conflict of interest that might breach the duty of loyalty, courts are unlikely to find a breach of the duty of care.

call An option in which one investor acquires the right, but not the obligation, to buy an underlying asset from another investor for a specified price during a specified period of time.

cap A contract that limits the amount the interest rate on a floating rate loan can increase, either annually or over the life of the loan.

clearinghouse In the futures market, a facility that oversees transactions on a daily basis. The clearinghouse confirms trades made each day, values each contract in every account at the end of every day and readjusts the cash balance of each trader's margin account accordingly, and insures performance of all of the futures contracts.

collateralized mortgage obligation (CMO) An instrument created to address the risk of prepayment in mortgage-backed securities. Investors are divided into successive maturity groups, called *tranches*, which receive principal payments in relation to different maturities. The higher-priority tranches face the lowest risk of prepayment, because they receive payments before the lower-priority tranches. Thus, a CMO can create high-priority classes that have little prepayment risk.

commissions Fee paid to the broker for buying and/or selling securities or futures contracts.

commodities Staple items such as wool, sugar, soybeans, pork, copper, gold, and other agricultural or industrial products that are traded on a commodity exchange.

contango The reverse of *backwardation* where the current price for future delivery (i.e., the futures price) is higher than the current spot price of an item.

contraction risk The risk that when interest rates fall, large numbers of homeowners may refinance their mortgage loans.

corporate credit spread risk The risk that the cost of financing will change due to changed perceptions about the credit risk of the issuer.

counterparty Term used for either of two parties who agree to enter into a direct financial contract, such as a swap transaction.

covered call A call option sold (written) for which the seller owns the underlying asset.

credit risk The risk that a party will default on his or her contract.

currency swap A swap that allows a party receiving payments based on one currency to exchange these for payments based on another currency. Currency swaps are thus a way of eliminating (or exploiting) differences between international capital markets.

dealer One who buys and sells securities and maintains an inventory of such securities. (*Brokers*, on the other hand, act as agents and do not necessarily keep their own inventory.)

deductible The amount of an insured loss that must be borne by the insured before the insurance takes effect. This concept applies to options in the same way as to health or other insurance policies. For example, a put option with a strike price of $70 per share on a stock that is currently trading at $73 per share has a built-in deductible amount of $3 per share.

derivative A financial instrument that derives its value from a more basic financial instrument. For example, an option on a stock (a basic form of derivative) derives its value from the underlying stock. Derivatives can be used to either increase or decrease risk.

director A person appointed or elected to manage and direct the affairs of a corporation. A director has a fiduciary duty to the corporation.

diversification A method of decreasing risk by spreading investments among different asset categories, such as stocks and bonds, and different companies in different industries within the stock category.

duty of loyalty The legal duty of a fiduciary to act for the exclusive benefit of those whose money is being managed—not for the benefit of the fiduciary personally or for any other party.

embedded option An option within another security. For example, home mortgages usually include an embedded option allowing the homeowner to prepay the principal without any penalty.

equity swap An agreement to swap an equity, for example by exchanging a fixed stream of cash flows for a varying stream of cash flows tied to the performance of a specific stock or stock market index.

exchanges Associations organized to provide a marketplace for purchasers and sellers of securities. Examples include the New York Stock Exchange, New York Commodities Exchange, and the Chicago Board of Trade.

exercise price The price provided for in an option contract at which the underlying security can be bought (for a call) or sold (for a put) on or before the expiration date of the option. Also referred to as *strike price.*

exercising (an option) The actual purchase or sale of the underlying asset of an option; American-style options can be exercised at any time before expiration; European-style options can be exercised only at the time of their expiration.

exit plan A financial plan to stop losses once they begin to occur, before they can grow so large as to exceed the comfortable limits of an organization.

extension risk Risk that, when interest rates increase, homeowners will hold on to their lower-interest loans longer so that prepayments will decrease.

face value The value appearing on the face of a certificate of a fixed-income security (such as a bond, note, or mortgage) that represents the amount due upon maturity of the security.

fiduciary A person responsible for investing his or her company's money or the money of others. Fiduciaries have a duty to act exclusively for the benefit of those they represent.

financial engineering   The use of financial instruments, such as derivatives, to obtain the desired mix of risk and return.

floater   A type of CMO tranche whose return will decrease as the index interest rates (such as LIBOR) fall and increase as they rise.

foreign currency risk   Risk that the value (i.e., exchange rate) of a foreign currency will change adversely in relation to the value of domestic currency. Also called *exchange-rate risk.*

forward contract   An agreement requiring the delivery of a certain quantity of a currency or other asset by a specified date in the future at a price agreed upon at the time of contracting.

future value   The estimated value at a future date of a present sum of money, based on appropriate interest rates.

futures commission merchant (FCM)   A futures broker.

futures contract   An agreement requiring the delivery of a certain quantity of an item by a specified date in the future at a price agreed upon at the time of contracting. Futures contracts differ from forward contracts in that they are traded on an organized exchange with standardized terms.

hedging   A strategy to protect against losses due to fluctuations in market prices. Hedging with derivatives involves avoiding risks rather than taking risks—the opposite of taking risk through speculation.

in the money   An option with intrinsic value. A call option is in the money when its exercise price is less than the price of the underlying security. A put option is in the money when its exercise price is greater than the price of the underlying security.

interest   The cost of borrowing money. Compensation for the use or forbearance of money.

interest-only strip (IO)   A tranche of a pass-through security which gives the holder the right to receive a portion of every interest payment, but not of principal payments.

interest rate risk   The risk that interest rates will change adversely. For example, the value of a bond decreases when interest rates increase.

interest rate swaps   A swap which allows a party receiving payments based on one measure, such as fixed interest rate to exchange these for payments based on another measure, such as a variable rate (often called a "floating" rate), or vice-versa.

intrinsic value (of an option)   For options which are "in the money," the mathematical difference between the market price of the underlying asset and the strike price of an option contract. This is the value the option would have if it were exercised immediately.

inverse floater   A type of CMO tranche whose return will increase as the index interest rates (such as Libor) fall, and decrease as they rise.

legal risk   The risk that a contract (such as a financial derivative contract) will not be enforced.

leverage   The ratio of the amount of money represented by an investment to the amount of money actually invested. With a high level of leverage, one experiences large gains or losses as though a much larger amount was invested. Leverage can increase the risk of large losses just as it increases the opportunity for large gains.

LIBOR (London interbank offered rate)   For banks that deal in Eurodollars, the rate that large international banks with excellent credit ratings charge each other for loans.

margin   An investor's cash deposit with a brokerage firm which acts as collateral for leveraged investments. For example, the investor may need to deposit only $1,000 in a margin account as collateral for a contract with a notional value of $10,000.

margin requirements   The minimum amount of cash a brokerage firm requires in a margin account to permit particular investments.

market risk   The risk that an asset (or an instrument such as a derivatives contract) will decrease in value with changes in market conditions, such as changes in interest and currency rates or fluctuations in equity and commodity prices.

marking to market   The process of recalculating (*marking*) the value of a contract according to the current market price.

mortgage derivative   A financial instrument that derives its value from mortgage pools, such as mortgage-backed pass-through securities or collateralized mortgage obligations.

mutual fund   A fund managed by a regulated investment company which pools the resources of individuals and makes investments on their behalf. Capital for the mutual fund is raised through the sale of interests in the fund, and the funds are then invested in securities.

Nikkei   The Japanese stock exchange.

operational risk   The risk that loss will occur due to inadequate management and oversight structure.

option   The right to buy (call) or the right to sell (put) an asset at a specified price within a fixed period of time.

out of the money   An option with no intrinsic value, but which may have some time value. A call option is out of the money when its exercise price is greater than the price of the underlying security. A put option is out of the money when its exercise price is less than the price of the underlying security.

over-the-counter (OTC) market   A market without a centralized exchange where trading is normally done via computers and telephone lines, coordinated through broker-dealers.

pass-through securities   Financial instruments that are collateralized by a pool of mortgages underlying the securities. Individual mortgagees make payments on their mortgages to the mortgage-pool fund, and the payments are passed through on a pro rata basis to the security holders. The pooled mortgages decrease the risk of default. (*Fully modified pass-throughs* are those where interest and principal payments are paid to the investor on time, whether or not individual borrowers default on their mortgages.)

pension fund   A fund set up, typically by corporations or unions, to pay pension benefits to employees after they retire.

portfolio   The collection of all securities (including stocks, bonds, derivatives, etc.) held by an individual or institution.

portfolio theory   An approach to investing that analyzes methods by which, through diversified portfolios, an optimal balance of risk and return can be reached.

present value   The estimated value today of a future sum of money, discounted at an appropriate interest rate.

principal   The capital or face amount of a debt or other obligation upon which interest accrues.

principal-only strip (PO)   A tranche of a pass-through security that gives the holder the right to receive a portion of every principal payment, but not of interest payments.

prudent-investor rule   A rule that requires a fiduciary to discharge his or her duties with the care, skill, prudence, and diligence under the circumstances then prevailing that a prudent person acting in like capacity and familiar with such matters would use in the conduct of an enterprise of like character and with like aims.

put   An option by which one investor acquires the right, but not the obligation, to sell an underlying asset to another investor for a specified price during a specified period of time.

real estate mortgage investment conduits (REMICs)   A special entity created to receive all the mortgage payments of a mortgage pool. Such entities were allowed by the Tax Reform Act of 1986.

repackaged asset   Part of an underlying asset that has been financially engineered into a variety of subdivided forms—each new investment may be more suitable for the needs of a particular investor than the underlying asset taken as a whole.

risk   The uncertainty associated with financial investments that actual returns could be lower than expected or potential returns.

risk management   The process of determining the optimal balance of risk and return for an organization or individual, entering into investments that will attain that optimal balance, and continually monitoring and evaluating the investments.

selling short   Selling shares of a stock that the investor does not own, but which a broker lends to the investor. This will be profitable when the stock price falls, since the investor will then purchase the stock at a price lower than that at which the investor sold it.

shareholder   A person who owns shares of stock (equity) in a corporation.

shorting against the box   The same as selling short, but the investor does own the stock and keeps the original stock in his or her account. Similar to a covered option, this position involves less risk than a straight short sale, since the stock in the investor's account can be used to satisfy the short position.

speculation   Taking risk, in hope of return, by buying or selling assets in hopes of profiting from market fluctuations. This is the opposite of reducing risk through hedging.

spot price   The current cash price for immediate delivery of goods.

spread   The difference between the price or value of one contract and the price or value of another similar contract. For example, a bank may have contracts to borrow money at the rate of 5 percent, and to lend money at the rate of 8 percent; the spread is the 3 percent difference.

standardized contracts   Contracts traded freely and publicly (as opposed to negotiated individually), with standardized quantities and dates.

stock   An instrument that provides the holder an equity, or ownership, interest in a corporation.

stock-index futures   Contracts requiring each party to make or receive payments based on the value of a standardized quantity of the underlying stock index on a specified date in the future.

straddle   A strategy where a put and a call, on the same asset with the same or very similar exercise price and expiration date, are either both purchased or both sold. When both are purchased, the investor gains when the value of the underlying asset increases or decreases. When both are sold, the investor gains when the asset value remains steady.

strike price   See **exercise price.**

swap   An agreement to exchange one set of cash flows for another. Swap agreements are often used to hedge against interest rate changes and fluctuations in foreign exchange rates. A typical example is an agreement to exchange fixed rate interest payments for variable rate interest payments on the same principal amount.

swaptions   An option to enter into a swap agreement.

synthetic bond   A virtual bond created by purchasing a bond with a good interest rate in one country and using a currency swap to transfer the payments to a currency of a different country. This creates the same effect as purchasing a bond in the second country. It is useful where the interest rates are higher in the first country, and the currency exchange rate between the countries is more or less stable.

synthetic futures An equivalent to a future created by buying a call and selling a put (a long position) or buying a put and selling a call (a short position) on the same underlying asset and with the same exercise price and expiration date. This strategy is useful when actual futures contracts are not available.

systemic risk Risk that an entire market will move generally in an adverse direction. This risk cannot be eliminated by diversification, but it can be hedged.

time value The market value of an option resulting from the probability that it will gain in value over time, before the expiration date. The more time there is before expiration, the greater the time value of the option.

trader's option The temptation (option) of a professional trader to delay reporting career threatening losses to his or her employer, and instead to make high-risk investments in hopes of quickly gaining back the losses.

tranche A part or slice of payments received by a mortgage-pool entity and paid out to the investor.

Treasury bond futures Futures contracts tied to U.S. Treasury bond rates that are used to lock in current interest rates or to speculate on future rates.

Treasury rate guarantee (TRY) Investments in Treasury securities whose value rises if interest rates rise. This is a type of interest rate hedge that allows a company that's issuing debt to protect itself against interest rate fluctuations—an increase in the cost of financing is offset by an increase in the value of the Treasuries.

trustee A person who holds certain property in trust for others.

ultra vires An act beyond the legal power or authority of the organization.

uncovered call (naked call) Call options sold (written) for which the seller does not own the underlying asset.

underlying asset The asset specified in a derivatives contract from which the contract derives its value.

variable rate An interest rate that changes along with a specified index (such as LIBOR, U.S. T-bills, etc.).

volatility The extent to which the price of an asset fluctuates. An asset with greater volatility experiences larger price swings. The higher the volatility of a stock, the more expensive are options on that stock.

Index